THE LESSON OF
JAPANESE ARCHITECTURE

165 PHOTOGRAPHS

JIRO HARADA
of the Imperial Household Museum, Tokyo

EDITED BY C. G. HOLME

DOVER PUBLICATIONS, INC.
NEW YORK

Published in Canada by General Publishing Company, Ltd., 30 Lesmill Road, Don Mills, Toronto, Ontario.
Published in the United Kingdom by Constable and Company, Ltd.

This Dover edition, first published in 1985, is an unabridged and slightly corrected republication of the work originally published by The Studio Ltd., London, in 1936 under the title *The Lesson of Japanese Architecture*.

Manufactured in the United States of America
Dover Publications, Inc., 31 East 2nd Street, Mineola, N.Y. 11501

Library of Congress Cataloging in Publication Data

Harada, Jiro.
    The lesson of Japanese architecture.

    Originally published: London : Studio, 1936.
    1. Architecture, Domestic—Japan. 2. Gardens, Japanese. 3. Architectural practice—Japan. I. Holme, C. Geoffrey (Charles Geoffrey), 1887-1954. II. Title.
NA7451.H26   1985   728.3'7'0952   84-21241
ISBN 0-486-24778-3

THIS VOLUME

is not intended to contain a complete history of Japanese architecture, nor to furnish a technical treatment of the construction of Japanese houses. It aims merely to afford, by means of illustrations, a glimpse of the exterior and interior of buildings, as they exist in Japan to-day. By such a glimpse it is hoped the reader may obtain some ideas, however vague, some hints, however slight, which may prove useful in the solution of the vital problem of improving living conditions—a problem which now confronts every serious-minded man and woman all over the world.

PUBLISHER'S NOTE, 1985

The lasting value of the volume republished here is in its irreplaceable collection of high-quality photographs of opulent Japanese homes and gardens as they appeared in the 1930s. Harada's brief text dealing with the practice of Japanese architects and builders through the centuries is also meritorious, although it is sometimes so concise as to run the risk of oversimplification and is tinged here and there with that special insularity fostered by the leaders of Japan during the period of military expansion.

Unfortunately the English version of Harada's useful summary was disfigured in the original 1936 edition by a number of typographical errors and inconsistencies. In the present edition an effort has been made to correct such gross errors as "Isumo" for Izumo, "Stalk" for Stork, and the like. Certain pervasive inconsistencies, however, have proved too troublesome to correct, and the reader's indulgence is requested for the variation in spelling and hyphenation in such words as "nationalization"/"nationalisation" and "chaseki"/"cha-seki" and for the widespread incompleteness of the macrons on Japanese long ō and ū. Certain old-fashioned transliterations, such as "Uyeno" for Ueno and "Hongwanji" for Honganji, not being actually errors, have been retained.

Lastly, it should be recalled that such terms as "now" and "recently" in the text refer to 1936. No updating has been attempted to take into account damage during World War II or subsequent restoration. Thus, for instance, the original structure of Nagoya Castle, "in an excellent state of preservation" in 1936, was totally destroyed in 1945, the present ferroconcrete reconstruction dating from only 1959.

CONTENTS

LIST OF ILLUSTRATIONS

DIAGRAMS AND PLANS

HISTORIC JAPANESE BUILDINGS

THE EXTERIOR

THE EXTERIOR (*continued*)

THE EXTERIOR (*continued*)

THE INTERIOR

THE LESSON OF
JAPANESE ARCHITECTURE

THE lesson of Japanese architecture for the Western world may be sum-
marised briefly as standardisation, variety in unity, conformity to a mode of
living, connection with nature, simplicity and, of course, usefulness to purpose.
These qualities are combined together in the traditional buildings of Japan.
Modern Western architects are not blind to the value of some of these qualities.
They have not yet arrived, however, at a solution of their own. Their solutions
are for the most part one-sided. It may be that from the study of a complete
and mature form of structure, which offers in detail some amazing likenesses
to their own efforts, they may find the clues they need. In the past the
interaction of these cultures widely removed in distance and spirit has not been
happy. The first impact of Eastern art on the West resulted in a connoisseur-
ship not always well-founded, and in a form of mixed decoration, trivial at best,
hideous at worst. Such was the *Chinoiserie* of the eighteenth century in which
the decorative motifs of Chinese art were adapted to the frivolous purposes of
an aristocratic age and a rococo style : and, being used subsequently in
commercial production, became in the following century a convention as hard
to escape from as ugly to look at. The architecture of the Far East was
symbolised in the Western mind by the pagoda : a form so peculiar that it
could only be used for some such spectacular or occasional purpose as an
exhibition or a firework display.

In other words the West for a long time thought of the East simply as a
source of entertaining oddities : or, if its admiration was deeper, it served little
purpose. A new phase, however, began in the nineteenth century when Japanese
prints found their way westwards and into the hands of those who were search-
ing for a new conception of art and were dissatisfied with the vulgar realism
and vulgar romance of the time. The influence of the Japanese print was
much healthier. Made known by the brothers de Goncourt in France, and
sifting through to the Anglo-Saxon world, it brought, with something of a
shock, a realization of the value of a formal or decorative treatment of subject
matter and an unaccustomed freedom in the use of colour. The excellent
paintings of Whistler are one evidence of this healthy influence which became
merged in the whole tendency of Western painting so much so that it could
no longer be detected as a separate and undigested element in it. The
corresponding effect on other arts was not at first so happy. The " Art
Nouveau " of the 1890's attempted to use natural forms, that is to say, prin-
cipally plant or vegetable forms in a way similar to that of the Japanese
craftsman ; but the results did not live up to the aim and the Art Nouveau

remains like pre-Raphaelitism, a movement that led nowhere and became meaningless.

These ups and downs are sufficient evidence of the tricky nature of enthusiasms for a foreign culture, and of course one could cite equal and even greater confusion produced in the East by the imitation of the West. To copy externals generally leads on the wrong road. To apply principles, however, is a different matter, more difficult to do, but essential to the living character of what is produced. Thus, even in the Art Nouveau period there was some feeling for the basic simplicity of Japanese architecture, and in the work of Viennese architects especially, who have contributed to the making of a characteristic twentieth-century architecture in the West.

Already, therefore, Japanese architecture has taught us something and when it has not directly taught us, there are likenesses because of a likeness in principle. It remains to make full use of these principles to distinguish between what can be adapted and what cannot be adapted, and to resolve some of our doubts and difficulties by reference to the Japanese solution.

We look round our landscape and what do we see? Here and there an old house built of local materials, mellowed by age and merging naturally into the landscape. Then we shall see small bungalows, with bright pink tiles, as gaudily coloured and incongruous as they can be. Some of these will imitate the appearance of old cottages but with a stagey effect because materials and structure are not the same. Here and there, perhaps, our eye will light on a " modern " house, a cube with horizontal windows, sharp corners and flat roof. We may be inclined to feel that this is the real form of architecture for modern life in its simplicity, its ample window room, etc., but at the same time the eye is offended and dissatisfied with the *aggressiveness* of the shape, with a sort of uncompromising bleakness which seems to decree that it is and always will be a stranger in the place where it finds itself. It wars with the landscape, just as the fake manor houses and gaudy bungalows do : and the more there are of them the more uneasy does the effect become. The spirit of the country disappears, leaving only the dreary appearance of not quite town, not quite country. The new house with its factory-like rigidity seems to bring all the restlessness and pre-occupations of the city with it ; and in the very act of escaping from the city we are once more building it up around us.

In this matter we have much to learn from the tradition of Japan where nature comes first : and the architect does not set out to dominate or destroy the surroundings of the house, but to render homage to them. The delight in and sympathy with nature entails a kind of camouflage. The thatched roofs, the wooden walls are carefully planned so that they modestly conceal themselves, and thus a cluster of Japanese houses seen from a distance in rural surroundings seems like a wood or a natural growth rather than a town which has come to destroy the country.

This is a matter of effect—but is it not important? We pay too little heed to the influence of architecture on the mind and are too readily satisfied with the most obvious answers to questions of utility. The Japanese, living on a comparatively small island, have to face the problem of numbers as we have, but they have a greater regard for privacy. To make the house a part of nature is one aspect of this regard. Another is to plan the house in relation to its immediate surroundings so that even if it is close to other houses it retains some mystery, some special charm because of the way in which a view is obstructed or open, and of relations that are deliberately planned. Thus the garden of the Japanese house comes right up to the windows, small space is made to look large because it conceals something from sight, and from the sliding panel of the living-room window one steps to the bank of a tiny stream that runs beneath it as if you were in the depth of a forest.

This may sound like a deliberate rusticness and nothing else; but the Japanese reserve for the interior the precision and simplicity which they know so well how to use. Perhaps here, the Western architect has most clearly approached to the Japanese idea. The rooms are devoid of detail but not bare. The clean lines and the absence of furniture without any relation to the room give an impression of restfulness. Built-in cupboards allow of the storing away of household goods not in use. A recess contains a work of art which thus acquires a special importance. Sliding panels permit of the room being thrown entirely open to the outer light and air; or of being combined when need be with another to make one large room. Though even here the Japanese do not forget the value of contrast and, to emphasise the pleasure one may derive from strictly geometrical proportions, one rough and unsmoothed support is again a reminder of the natural principle.

This simplicity of form and proportion is one from which the West can still learn much. Two things are to be noted—firstly that it is essentially unobtrusive —it is not a dogma or theory on the part of the architect, but a modest method of finding the term for the greatest convenience of the inhabitants and for giving them pleasure by the quiet refinement of their surroundings. Secondly, it represents economy, of materials, of space, and turns this economy into a virtue.

The Japanese have already learnt and applied the methods of standardization and we are still behind them as far as architecture is concerned, in this respect. The unit is the mat, a certain number of which cover the floor, and thus the number of mats governs the size of the room and so the size of the whole house according to a known and fixed measurement. Faced as we are with the problem of mass production, we can learn from this the possibility of producing a house of standardised parts which nevertheless allow scope for variety in arrangement. The Japanese never forget the necessity of balance; it is an essential feature of their civilisation and thus, though keenly aware of the value of formulæ, of purely mathematical solutions, of the value of repetition and of precision, they show that this is not everything by planning deliberate irregularities to break a uniform and monotonous regularity. Fences and walls, for example, are made in many different shapes to this end.

In fact Japanese architecture is devised not for the sake of architecture, but for the sake of living. The passion for beauty is not limited to the works of a few famous artists—it is extended to the ordinary course of day to day existence. The part played by the famous tea-ceremony, a sort of ritual in which host and guest meet under the inspiring and refining influence of a common worship of beauty, with gestures that match the occasion, introducing a sense of profound philosophy into the meeting of friends, has been an important one. It has governed the grave attention given to the shaping of the house and its contents as the expression of a philosophy, even of a religion. Perhaps in the West we are too obtuse to a practice of this kind, which, however, makes our " machine for living in " seem somewhat crude and void of any real satisfaction. There is more in it than this, say the Japanese, with their mature civilisation behind them. True simplicity is not to be so easily attained. Much as they have cultivated the utilitarian method they have never lost sight of its relation to the mind.

Equally important, then, with the practical advantages to be appreciated in the illustrations which Mr. Harada has made it a labour of love to collect and describe, is the state of mind a Japanese building represents. Behind it is the importance of Shintoism, creating a code of art which may be defined as consisting in quiet taste, in a beauty that is not all on the surface, but is to be discovered by degrees, in simplicity without severity, in the avoidance of what is gaudy, crude or ostentatious. It is, in fact, a form of good manners, and how many of our Western houses will pass this test? At bottom, then, failure to do so is the trouble with our hasty and pretentious schemes for " housing the masses," for " improvement " which adds to existing ugliness. Japanese architecture is not to be considered as an exotic or eccentric importation, but a reminder of good manners when such is badly wanted.

THE EDITOR.

Stages in the development of the tenchi-kongen, the earliest known type of Japanese building. (See the opposite page.)

A SHORT
HISTORICAL SURVEY

A brief historical survey of Japanese architecture may give the reader the necessary background for the appreciation of Japanese houses. Though there are different ways of classifying the architectural history of Japan, it may conveniently be divided into the following seven periods :

I.—The Pre-Buddhist Period, extending down to the official introduction of Buddhism into Japan in A.D. 552.

II.—The first Period of Chinese Influence, extending from 553 to the rise of the Fujiwara clan in 889, thus including the Asuka (552-644), Nara (645-780) and Early Heian (781-885) periods.

III.—The First Nationalization, lasting through the Late Heian period (898-1185).

IV.—The Second Period of Chinese Influence, which lasted through the Kamakura (1186-1333) and the Muromachi (1334-1572) periods.

V.—The Second Nationalization, which occurred in the Momoyama (1573-1602), and Edo periods—Early Edo (1603-1680), Middle Edo (1681-1778) and Late Edo (1779-1867).

VI.—The Period of European Influence, including the Meiji and Taisho eras (1868-1926).

VII.—The Present Period, 1927.

I.—Pre-Buddhist Period.

In primitive ages the Japanese race lived in caves as in other countries, but when they were sufficiently advanced to build houses they built wooden huts of the simplest kind which developed the most primitive type of building known as *tenchi-kongen*. It consisted of two posts set in the ground supporting at the top a ridge pole, to each end of which were fastened two rafters sloping to the ground. To these rafters a number of beams were tied horizontally to support a thatch which served for roof as well as walls. Later this whole structure was elevated by introducing walls on four sides and a raised floor —a simple type of house with gabled roof.

This form of construction was first adopted for shrines, for they were to be the living houses for the spirits of the dead, for whom an offering of food was made. This oldest type of shrine is known as *O-yashiro* and is still preserved in the shrine at Izumo. This was later modified, deviating slightly from living houses and forming a special type for shrines, and the types known as *Otori* and *Sumiyoshi* and still later *Shimmei*, came into existence. The *Otori* type may be seen in the shrine at *Otori* ; the *Sumiyoshi* type is still perpetuated in the Sumiyoshi shrine near Osaka ; the *Shimmei* type finds its perfect prototype in the Imperial Shrine at Ise which is rebuilt every twenty years exactly in the same style, faithful to the minutest detail. These are the four early types of Shinto architecture, which reproduced in a large measure the Imperial Palaces of the time. We know that they were somewhat different from ordinary dwelling-houses, for documents show that the common people were forbidden to use certain decorations on the roof known as *chigi* (the horn-like projection of timbers at each gable-end) and *katsuogi* (a row of weight-blocks of wood placed on the ridge at right angles to it) in the reign of the Emperor Yuryaku (A.D. 456-479). Practically all the shrines retain these peculiarities on the roof. There are no less than 140,000 shrines throughout the country, nearly every ancient grove of dense trees harbouring a shrine, each with one or more *torii*—a simple framework consisting of two horizontal beams supported by two posts set in the ground—serving as their symbol. These shrines are all built of wood—with very few recent exceptions introduced in reinforced concrete built in the traditional style—and are constantly being rebuilt in the same original simple style. Not only do these shrines represent the primitive type of ancient Imperial Palace and suggest common dwelling-houses, but they stand to-day as sacred symbols of the ideals of the people, ever reminding them of the houses of the gods, making them realise the presence of the spirit of the dead, and transporting them to the days of yore when their ancestors lived simple lives close to nature. No one can help being deeply impressed by these shrines—impressed by their extreme simplicity and something sacred which it seems to breathe. This simplest form of architecture is in perfect harmony with ancient trees suggesting primeval forest, and is profoundly impressive. What the noted priest Saigyo wrote of the Imperial shrine at Ise in a thirty-one syllabled poem—" I know not what is within, but I am in tears with gratitude "—is true. The sentiment is echoed in the heart of every Japanese visiting the shrine, all being deeply struck by the sanctity of the place. Real Japan, the old and true Nippon, seems to dwell there, speaking to the people in the silent language of the past of the eternity of beauty and truth in nature.

Since the invasion of Korea by the Empress Jingo Kogu, presumably in the third century A.D., Japan was in intimate communication with the peninsular kingdom, which doubtless influenced Japanese architecture. It is recorded that one of the Korean Kings presented to the Japanese Emperor five kinds of pigments which are supposed to have been used for colouring buildings. It is also recorded that the Emperor Nintoku (313-399) did away with palace decorations at the time of a famine during his reign, and that he ascended " lofty structure " which is mentioned also in connection with the reign of the two succeeding Emperors. It may be known from this that the palaces at that time were no longer of the simplest form. However, the progress of palace architecture was greatly retarded by the custom which then existed of changing the seat of the Imperial Court at the death of each Emperor. This was not at all conducive to establishing any elaborate or substantial style of building. Real progress did not come, therefore, until this custom was abandoned with the establishment of the Court at Nara in 708, where it remained until it was removed to Nagaoka in Yamashiro province to remain there for ten years and later to Kyoto ; here the capital of the Empire remained almost eleven centuries until it was finally removed to Yedo, now called Tokyo, in 1868.

II.—First Period of Chinese Influence.

With the official introduction of Buddhism into Japan in 552 from Korea the architecture, as well as other branches of art, was greatly changed. Following the introduction there came in 588 a large number of temple builders, painters, tile-makers and other artisans from Korea. Temples were built on a grand scale under the leadership of Prince Shotoku, who is worshipped in Japan as the patron saint of art and culture. Such temples as the Hokoji (later called Gangoji), the Shitennōji, Hokkiji, Hōrinji and Hōryuji were established. The last mentioned was completed in 607 and still preserves some of the original buildings—the Kondō (the main sanctuary) the five-storied pagoda, the gatehouse, and a part of the corridor. Nothing remains of the original Hokoji building, or of the Shitennōji ; but the Hokkiji and Hōrinji each still preserves an original three-storied pagoda. What remains of these temples to this day eloquently speaks of the grandeur of scale and the magnificence of the buildings. Though built by the aid of Koreans, these buildings show the influence of the Six Dynasties of China, with pillars with entasis, arms in the cloud-design (*kumohijiki*) of the brackets supporting the eaves, and *kaeru-mata* (beam supports). Though we have no specimen left of the living-houses of the common people of the time, these, it may be supposed, cannot have been changed very much by foreign influences. The residences of the aristocrats were the ones most affected. Naturally, of course, immigrants from the Continent would have built their dwellings in their native style.

In the Nara period the influence of the T'ang culture was irresistible. The capital was laid out on a magnificent scale after the Chinese plan ; the Imperial Palace buildings had roofs of green-glazed tiles and pillars painted red. No less than twenty original buildings of the eighth century stand to-day, chief among them being the West Kondō of the Kairyuōji Temple, the Hokkedō of the Todaiji Monastery, the Saiinjikido, the Yumedono (Dream Hall) and Dempodo of the Hōryuji monastery, the main building of the Shin Yakushiji, the Kondō and Kōdō (Lecture Hall) of the Tōshōdaiji temple, and a few repositories in the *azegura* style, the most important of which is the Shōsōin at Nara (see pages 57 to 59). The Shōsōin, which dates from about 752, was built of triangular timbers laid horizontally one on top of another, crossed at the corners like a log-cabin, making the interior surface smooth and the exterior corrugated. This type of treasure-house may have already been in existence in the preceding period, though we have no extant example. The temples under the T'ang influence assumed a still greater grandeur of scale as may be seen from what remains of the Todaiji Monastery in Nara completed about 750.

Among other features, the decoration on the brackets became less profuse, their arms in the cloud-design disappearing or leaving faint traces only on the underside. The exterior of the temples was painted in red oxide of lead and the interior in full colour, the peculiarity of the decoration of this period being the gradation of different shades of colour known as *ungen*.

Even after the new regime—Early Heian period—was begun with the removal of the capital to Kyoto, the influence of the T'ang culture still continued to be felt but the people became more discriminating than before. The rise of the two great esoteric Buddhist sects—*Tendai* and *Shingon*—vitally changed religious architecture. Hitherto the temples had been built in cities and on level ground, but now they came to be constructed on mountain tops. The *Tendai* established a monastery on Hiyeizan, a high mountain near Kyoto, and the *Shingon* on distant Kōyasan, a plateau surrounded by mountains. Both of these monasteries are still maintained as the main seats of their respective sects, though none of the original buildings now remains. It was impossible to arrange the buildings of the temples symmetrically on mountains as the custom was on the level ground. Freedom was allowed not only in the arrangement of the buildings, but also in the construction of individual structures. A part of the tiled floor was changed to a raised wooden floor for convenience in sitting. The main sanctuary and the five-storied pagoda of the Murōji temple, the former built about 848 and the latter in 824, are precious relics of this period. The pillars still show a slight entasis from the Asuka period. The palace, too, underwent a change : some of the buildings were given roofs of chamæcyparis bark, instead of glazed tiles, and otherwise modified, showing a tendency toward the style of the Period of Nationalisation which followed.

There was a movement to harmonise the faiths of Buddhism and Shinto, and this effort was manifested in shrine architecture. As a result of this effort, a certain curvature was introduced into the roof, showing a tendency toward elaboration, though this was conscientiously repulsed. As a consequence, the following four types were developed : (1) *Kasuga*, with a roof sloping from below the gable and over the entrance steps (the type is preserved in the Kasuga shrine of Nara) ; (2) *Nagare*, with the same plan as *Shimmei*, but with curves to the roofs and the front roof extended to cover the steps (an example, though not the original, may be seen at the Kamo shrine of Kyoto) ; (3) *Hachiman*, with two rooms, each with a roof over it (an example is furnished by the Usa Hachiman shrine of Kyushu) ; (4) *Hiye*, with roof extended to front and sides in the shape of *irimoya* with the back cut off (a prototype is to be seen at the Hiye shrine on the banks of Biwa Lake).

III.—Period of First Nationalisation.

The late Heian period (898-1185) was the age in which there was a great reaction against imported culture. For a time the custom of sending scholars to China for the purpose of study was stopped, after having been maintained for about 280 years. Left alone, Japan had time to discriminate and digest what she had taken in, and to reassert herself. It was the period in which art and literature flourished, full play having been given to the development of native taste. The people of the time welcomed the newly risen, easy-going faith of *Nembutsu* or the *Jōdo* sect, rather than the solemn and mystic *Tendai* and *Shingon* already referred to. Many large temples were established for the new sect, but it was natural that they should lack, as they did, the stability and grandeur of the older temples. Yet what is now regarded as true Japanese taste in architecture, as well as in other branches of art, was developed during this period. The art produced then was remarkable for grace and refinement; it lacked force and strength, but was full of dignity and elegance.

Among the temples built by the Emperors of this period mention may be made of the following six: the Hōshōji, Sonshōji, Seishōji, Saishōji, Yenshōji, and Enshōji, all of which were conspicuous for their great scale and elaborate decoration. Among those established by the Fujiwara aristocrats, who revelled in power, wealth and luxury, the most famous were the following: the Daigōji, Hōshōji, Byōdoin, Ryōgonji, Hōseiji, Hōjuji and Hōkōji. Among these the Hōseiji, built by Michinaga, was most magnificent, according to the documents, although nothing now remains of the original to prove it. Some of the important buildings now existing from this period may be enumerated below: the five-storied pagoda of the Daigōji, the Sanzen-in, the Lecture Hall of the Hōryuji Monastery, the main building of the Jōruriji, the Konjikidō of the Chūsonji, Byōdō-in (Phœnix hall), the Amidadō of the Hōkaiji, the Lecture Hall of the Kōryuji, etc. Most of these may be termed an Amida-dō (Hall for Amitabha) which came into existence with the rise of *Jōdo*, the new sect. One of their peculiarities was the absence of demarcation between the inner and outer sanctuaries within the temple building, thereby causing all the Buddhist images to be placed on the central altar (*Shumidan*), and another was the profuse decoration given to the interior to suggest *Jōdo* (Sanskrit, *Sukhavati*) the Buddhist paradise.

Not only did the aristocracy build temples—and they were so powerful and wealthy that many of them established separate family temples—but they also built their own mansions on an elaborate scale, developing a style known as *shinden-zukuri* (see page 56), which consisted of a number of rectangular buildings joined by long corridors, with a landscape garden on the south side containing a large pond with an island in it. Such was also the plan adopted for palace architecture. The houses of the common people remained simple with thatched roofs.

The four types of the previous period continued to exist for shrines, but a marked preference was shown for the *Kasuga* and *Nagare*, and minor buildings necessary in connection with festivals, etc., were added as accessory structures. Furthermore, other features were elaborated: corridors were substituted for the fences surrounding the shrine, and the simple *torii* was replaced by an eight- or four-post gate. As in the case of the mansions of the aristocrats, these structures were characterised by dignity, refinement and grace, reflecting the spirit of the age, and revealing the highly developed taste of the Japanese race.

IV.—Second Period of Chinese Influence.

With the establishment of the Shogunate at Kamakura in 1186, the political centre was shifted from Kyoto to Kamakura, the power being transferred from the aristocratic to the *samurai* (warrior) class, and the tendency of the age passing from grace and refinement to simplicity and vigour. Kamakura was so far removed geographically from Kyoto that in the earlier part of this period the aristocratic taste still continued to prevail in Kyoto, while the *samurai* taste was developed in Kamakura. But a little later the simplicity of the samurai found its way to Kyoto, while the refinement of the aristocrats pervaded Kamakura, thus interchanging the fashions of these two metropolises for a time. It was natural that the rise of the *samurai* class should affect the architecture of the period, for this meant the birth of a middle class which soon gained power and caused aristocratic taste to be superseded by democratic. In the previous period temples were built by wealthy individuals single-handed, but now that was no longer the case ; the necessary fund had to be raised by public subscription. Not only so, but there was a change in the style of architecture caused by the Zen sect of Buddhism.

Although the custom of sending cultural missions to China was dispensed with in 894, private intercourse was continued by merchants and Buddhist priests. The Zen sect of Buddhism was brought to Japan from Sung, spread among *samurai* and aristocrats, and was destined to influence all branches of art, including, of course, architecture. The Zen temples of Sung were reproduced in Japan and the style of these new buildings was called *Kara-yō* (Chinese style) in contradistinction to the *tenjiku-yō* (Indian style) which was imported into Japan earlier in the period and applied in the reconstruction of the main hall and the south gate-house of the Todaiji Monastery. The older style which continued to exist from the previous period was named *wa-yō* (Japanese style). These three styles existed side by side until the *wa-yō* and the *kara-yō* merged into one and developed a mixed style, while the *tenjiku-yō* failed to make much headway.

A brief comparison of these three styles will help to bring out their striking features. The *wa-yō* allowed great freedom in the planning of the temple and in the arrangement of the different buildings of the temples, while the *kara-yō* insisted, as in the case of the Buddhistic architecture first introduced from China in the seventh century, on their symmetrical arrangement. The *kara-yō* revived the tiled floor, discarding the raised wooden one of the *wa-yō*. The *kara-yō* increased the height of the altar, the ceiling, and the building itself. It established the custom of leaving the woodwork plain and of placing a single image of Buddha on the altar, instead of many, and otherwise simplifying the whole interior to have it conducive to Zen meditation—a great contrast to the profuse decoration of the *Jōdo* sect. However, in the *kara-yō* there was a certain increase of decorative details on the exterior : the brackets were no longer confined, as in the *wa-yō* to the top of the pillars, but were increased in number and introduced between the posts as well ; certain carved decorations came to be used for the gable-ends, and also on the ends

18

of beams, etc. The striking feature of the *tenjiku-yō* may be seen in the elaborate system of bracketing; the arms, projecting to the front of the pillars only, being often as many as seven, instead of two or three as in the *wa-yō*.

Mention may be made here of a few buildings dating from this period. The Fudō-dō of the Kōyasan Monastery, a square building with its graceful sweep of roof line; the main hall of the Rengeoin, of Kyoto, a long building with a corridor all around; the Tahōtō (two-storied stupa) at Ishiyama-dera Temple, one of the oldest and best of its type, and the beautifully proportioned three-storied pagoda of the Kofukuji Temple, Nara, are all in the *wa-yō*, though they are entirely different in shape. The Shari-den of the Engakuji Temple of Kamakura and the Jizōdō of the Shōfukuji Temple of Tokyo, represent the *kara-yō*, while the main hall and the south gate-house of the Todaiji Temple show the *tenjiku* style. The best example of the mixed style of *kara-yō* and *wa-yō* is the main building of the Kanshinji Temple, Kawachi; this mixed style was further developed and became the principal style in subsequent periods.

These influences did not confine themselves to Buddhist temples alone, but they extended also to Shinto shrines, some of which came to assume *irimoya* roofs.

The destruction of the Imperial Palaces by repeated fires and also the political disturbances that caused a division in the Imperial lineage between the north and south prevented us from having any reliable data concerning the architecture of the Imperial Palaces of this period. On the whole, however, the *shinden* style seems to have continued in favour with the aristocrats of Kyoto, while the *buke (samurai)* style, which was in the main the simplification of *shinden-zukuri*, was devised for the *samurai* class. It was customary in the *buke* style to surround the house with a ditch and fence. Instead of having many separate buildings joined by long corridors, as in the case of the *shinden* style, the *buke* style had many rooms under one roof, or groups of roofs joined together. The houses were thatched or shingled, there being hardly any evidence of tiles. This style finally evolved the *shoin* style of the Muromachi period which followed.

The Muromachi period also comes under the fourth division of architectural development—the period under the second Chinese influence. The power now went to the Ashikaga clan which lived at Muromachi in Kyoto. Kamakura being abandoned, Kyoto again became the political centre. The simple ways of the *samurai* were forgotten by the time Yoshimitsu, the third Ashikaga Shogun, began his life of luxury. Yoshimasa, the eighth Shogun, carried the fashion still further; he was a great patron of art, being himself a great devotee of *cha-no-yu*, or ceremonial tea based on Zen, which exerted a powerful influence on all forms of art. Its far-reaching effect cannot be overestimated. Powerful personages rivalled each other in building magnificent mansions for themselves, thus giving a stimulus to the development of painting, architecture, gardening, and the various branches of applied arts. The advancement of art in this period may be compared in importance to that of the Fujiwara regime in the Late Heian period.

This was followed by many wars which constitute the dark ages, yet the influence of the Ming culture, through Buddhist priests, was persistent. Towards the end of the period European merchant ships began calling at Japanese ports—Portuguese, followed by Spanish and English ships. Thus a European influence, though slight, began to be felt also.

While esoteric Buddhism still remained the religion of the Imperial Court and Shogunate, the spread of the Zen sect among the middle class made its influence felt not only on the literature, manners and customs, but also on architecture and other branches of the art of the time. Therefore, it was natural that *kara-yō* and the mixed style of *kara-yō* and *wa-yō* should thrive, as it did, the pure *wa-yō* and *tenjiku-yō* being much neglected. Such a tendency was extended even to the Shinto shrines. The *samurai* style, which originated at Kamakura, was perfected during the Muromachi period, resulting in the creation of a style known as *shoin-zukuri*. This style introduced into the dwelling houses the *tokonoma* (alcove), shelves on the wall, a fixed table by the window, sliding paper screens (*fusuma*), and wooden panels (*sugito*), both decorated generally with landscapes in monochrome, coffered ceilings, narrow verandahs, and an entrance room (*genkan*). As noted architectural examples built by the Shoguns of this period the Kinkakuji (gold pavilion) and the Ginkakuji (silver pavilion) may be mentioned. Among other temples of this period may be enumerated the East Kondo of the Kofukuji Temple, Nara, rebuilt in 1411, the five-storied pagoda of the same temple rebuilt in 1426, and the gate-house of the Tofukuji Temple of Kyoto. Among examples of shrines, the Kibitsu Jinsha, of Okayama, and the Takemigumari Jinsha of Kawachi may be mentioned.

V.—Second Nationalization.

With the downfall of the Ashikaga clan, the nation fell into disorder, but soon order was partially restored under Nobunaga, a great general who established a new regime—a short but significant regime, especially from the art standpoint—known as the Azuchi-Momoyama (Momoyama for short) period: 1573-1602. Nobunaga was loyal to the Court and built Imperial Palaces and repaired shrines, and Kyoto gradually regained its former aspect. He built his own magnificent castle on Azuchi hill overlooking Lake Biwa and gave the master painter, Kano Eitoku, a free hand to decorate its interior. The castle contained a seven-storied keep, about 100 feet high, and showed in many respects marked progress in the architecture of fortification. This splendid castle, with living apartments gorgeously decorated, was entirely destroyed by fire only about seven years after its completion.

Hideyoshi, when he rose to power, built some important structures among which the following may be mentioned-: Osaka Castle, the keep of which was recently restored in reinforced concrete; the Juraku Palace in Kyoto which was removed to Momoyama during his lifetime and a part of which now stands as the " Hiunkaku " in the compound of the Nishi Hongwanji Temple in the same city, and the Momoyama Castle. This Momoyama Castle

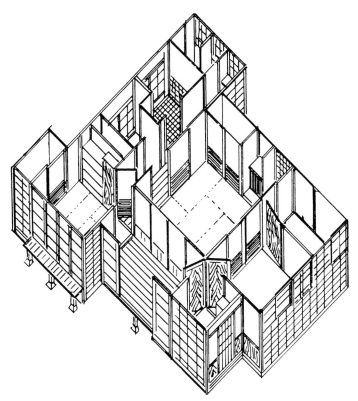

THE ORGANISATION
OF A TYPICAL
JAPANESE HOUSE

A. Entrance.   B. Tokonoma.
C. Chigai-dana (shelves in an alcove).
D. Main room.
EE. Subsidiary rooms.
F. Smaller guest-room with chairs.
G. W.C.   H. Bathroom.
I. Kitchen.   J. Passage.
K. Covered verandah.

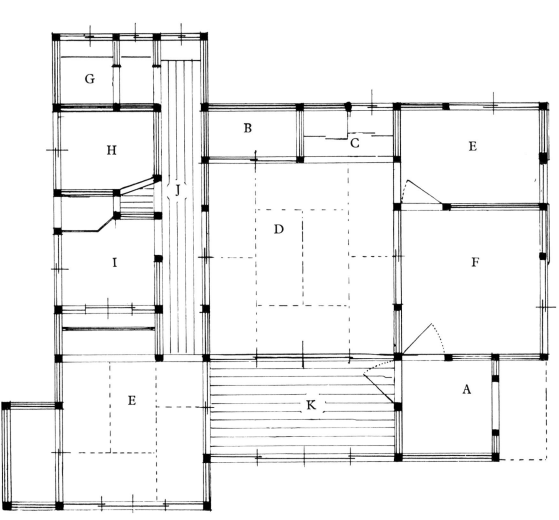

was an elaborate affair, and parts of which are still preserved as follows : the gate-houses of the Daitokuji temple, of the Hōkoku shrine, and of the Nishi Hongwanji Temple, and also the " Stork Chamber " of the last-mentioned temple, all in Kyoto. The Nagoya Castle, completed in 1611, famous for the pair of golden dolphins on the roof of the keep, remains in an excellent state of preservation, and contains a building from the Kiyosu Castle constructed in the previous period. Hideyoshi also built a temple named Hōkōji in Kyoto on a colossal scale, but it was burnt, rebuilt and finally destroyed by lightning. Among the temples and their accessory buildings, dating from this period, mention may be made of the following : the Zuiganji Temple at Matsushima, completed in 1609 ; the Kōndo of the Tōji Temple, rebuilt in 1606 ; the Founder's Hall (Kaisando), the mausoleum (Rei-oku), and the Front Gate of the Kōdaiji Temple, built in 1605 ; and the Imperial Messenger's Gate, built in 1590, at the Daitokuji Temple, Kyoto. Hideyoshi was a great hero and was mainly responsible for the grandeur and splendour in art known as the " Momoyama style." Though he was the central figure, it was essentially the age of the common people, full of masculine power, opposed to social classes and traditions. It was the spirit of the age to be bold, daring and free. This spirit was clearly reflected in the architecture as well as in other branches of the art and craft of the period.

It may be mentioned that Hideyoshi was a tea devotee, who utilized *cha-no-yu* for political ends, causing a great development of the *cha-seki* (tea room) architecture, which advocated simplicity and played an important part in the subsequent architectural history of Japan. Hitherto *cha-no-yu* was a sort of pastime for the upper classes, but now it entered into the life of the common people, having been popularized by the great tea-master, Rikyu. The development of this simple style of architecture was in interesting contrast to the gorgeous style formerly in vogue. Yet the simplicity shown in earlier types of Shinto shrines and *cha-seki* may be pointed out as similar and as expressing the fundamental ideas of Japanese architecture.

The shrines of this period were somewhat modified, and a style known as " *gongen-zukuri* " came into existence. In consisted of one building for the sanctuary, another in front for worshipping, and these two buildings joined together, formed between them an *ai-no-ma*, or sunken room paved with stone. This gave a complicated system of roofs ; hence the style is often called *yatsumune*, or " eight-roofed." A noteworthy example remaining from this period is the Kitano Jinsha completed in 1607.

European intercourse was opened at the end of the previous period and continued throughout this period, and as a consequence Christianity was spread with remarkable rapidity all over Japan, no less than half a million converts being made in fifty years, from 1549 to 1598. Though Christianity was partially prohibited by Hideyoshi in 1587, a number of Christian churches in a foreign style must have been built, though they left scarcely any influence on our architecture, not a single example now remaining.

Hitherto the development of Japanese architecture had been centred about

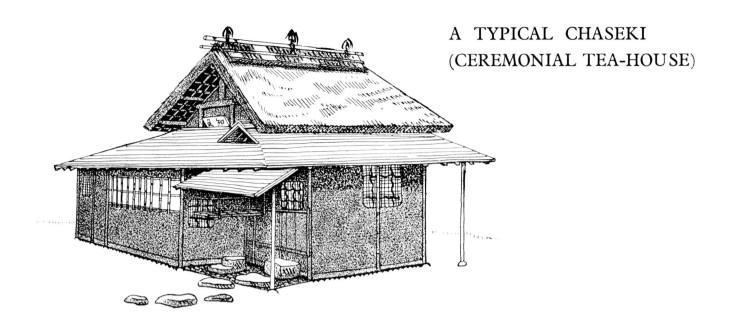

A TYPICAL CHASEKI
(CEREMONIAL TEA-HOUSE)

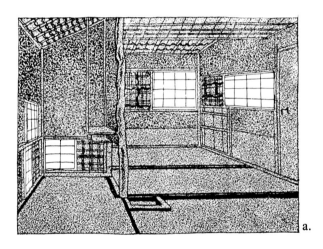

a.   b.

Above : The exterior and two interior views of a typical *chaseki* (Tea House). (*a*) Shows on the left a small square door used by the guests as an entry, etiquette demanding that they should enter on hands and knees as a sign that rank and station are set aside. To the right of it is a place for the host with shelves, and with a charcoal fire let into the floor. (*b*) On the left is the recess known as the *tokonoma* containing a single poem and a flower arrangement. The post of natural timber supporting the canopy is a compliment to nature's construction in contrast with man-made straight lines and planes.
Right : A rough plan (not to scale) of the floor space.

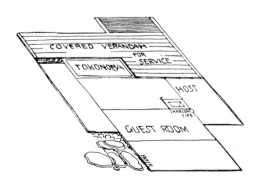

Buddhist temples, but now it took a different course—the attention of the people was turned more towards men and things directly connected with daily life, viz., castles, palaces, and dwelling houses. Such was the case with sculpture and painting as well ; instead of Buddhist statues the sculptors were engaged in carving *ramma* (a panel fitted between the beam above the partitions of rooms and the ceiling) and *kaeru-mata* (decorative supports of beams) ; instead of Buddhist images the artists devoted themselves to painting secular subjects on the sliding screens and ceilings. In no other period in Japanese history did architecture, sculpture and painting all co-operate in such perfect harmony as they did in the Momoyama period. The peculiarity of the architecture of this period was the disregard for traditional methods and the creation of a new style. The architects were not bound either by the native (*wa-yō*), the Chinese (*kara-yō*), the Indian (*tenjiku-yō*), or the mixed style. They were bent on devising original modes of expression, transcending them all. The *shoin-zukuri*, the style of dwelling house with a study, which was originated about the middle of the previous period, was now more fully developed. Since the Wars of Onin (1467-1477) the practice had become general of covering the entire floor in the Japanese house with *tatami* (wadded mats) ; of having gold sliding screens with paintings on ; of coffering the ceiling and decorating it with lacquer and pictorial painting ; of installing a *tokonoma* (alcove with a raised floor), and *chigai-dana* (shelves at uneven levels) in the main room. Among important relics of this class of architecture, mention may be made of the Sambōin Temple of Daigo and the Kanchi-in of the Tōji Temple of Kyoto, besides the " Hiunkaku " and the " Stork Chamber " of the Nishi Hongwanji already mentioned.

Because of the great influence exerted by *cha-no-yu* on architecture as a whole, mention may be made of some important tea masters who lived about this time and of the *chaseki* then built. Among these tea masters were Sen-no-Rikyu, Furuta Oribe, Hosokawa Tadaoki, Ota Yurakusai, Kobori Enshū, Katakiri Sekishū and Kanamori Sowa. They were not only masters of *cha-no-yu*, but also artists of great attainments, having designed *chaseki* (houses for *cha-no-yu*) and gardens as well. The following may be mentioned as some of the important *chaseki* built at this time and at the beginning of the Edo period ; the *chaseki* of the Shinjuan and Tsūsen-in, of the Daito-kuji Temple ; the Karakasatei and Shigure-tei, of the Kōdaiji Temple ; the Myōkian of Yamazaki, the Sekkai-tei of the Kinkakuji Temple, and various buildings of the Katsura and Shugakuin detached palaces.

The period of the second nationalization continued throughout the Edo period (1603-1867), when the Japanese were able to free themselves almost entirely from foreign influences. The culture of the Edo period was that of the common people, not of the aristocrats. Looking back we realize that in the sixth and seventh centuries the influences of the Sui and T'ang cultures strongly affected our civilization, and so greatly modified it that up the eighth century it was hardly anything but a transplantation of Chinese culture. From the ninth century nationalization began, and in the tenth our own culture was developed and maintained through the two centuries that followed, though it was confined to the aristocrats. The Sung and Yüan influences were felt from the thirteenth to the middle of the sixteenth century, while *cha-no-yu*, poetic dialogue (*ren-ga*) and *noh* drama helped to maintain and spread the native culture among the common people who were most active in reasserting themselves in the latter half of the sixteenth century and who carried the native culture still further in the three centuries that followed when popular Japanese literature and art—such as novels, plays, *haiku* (seventeen syllabled poems), and *ukiyoye* (genre paintings)—reached the height of their development.

Religious architecture of the Edo period remained somewhat stagnant, though earlier in the period the Obaku sect of Zen Buddhism was introduced into Japan from China and a temple built at Uji, the Mampukuji, which still remains. Yet Buddhism was by no means inactive : in the Hōreki era (1751-63) there were no less than 121,000 temples of the Jōdo sect, 81,000 of the Hokke sect, and 80,000 of the Hongwanji sect. The buildings were influenced by the spirit of the age, and grew more and more Japanese in style. The grandeur of the Momoyama period, however, gradually disappeared, and the long-continued peace had a tendency to make people conservative, weak, and concerned chiefly with non-essentials. All of this was reflected in the buildings of the period. Different styles of architecture lost their distinctive characteristics ; they were blended into each other, differences being revealed only in minor details, while architects remained conservative.

Noteworthy was the development, in this period, of the mausoleum, a complicated form of Shinto architecture of the *gongen-zukuri* style. Its most prominent examples are the shrines at Nikko, some of which were built in 1616-7 and the rest completed in 1634-6. There were other mausolea erected likewise for the spirit of the dead Tokugawa Shoguns, within the compound of the Zōjōji temple at Shiba and the Kwanyeiji Temple at Uyeno, both in Tokyo. When the spirit of the people was more active in the first part of this period, such large temples as the above-mentioned Zōjōji and the Kwanyeiji, five-storied pagoda of the Tōji Temple, Kyoto, and the Daibutsuden (Hall of Great Buddha), Nara, were built, and many neglected temples in Kyoto were either reconstructed or repaired.

As the study of Confucianism was encouraged by feudal lords, Confucian temples were built in various provinces throughout the country. In some instances similar Chinese edifices were copied, though on a small scale, but these buildings failed to make any lasting impression on Japanese architecture. Castles continued to be constructed, a notable example being the Edo castle, parts of which still remain in the Imperial Palace grounds. Another example is the Nijō castle of Kyoto which was begun in 1603 and completed in 1624 by the addition of various buildings from the Fushimi castle. The Nijo castle contains apartments which constitute the best specimens we have of *shoin-zukuri*, and which reflect the grandeur of the Momoyama period, as the people building them were still under the spell of its influence. The homes of the samurai were developed on a more or less definite plan : the lord's dwelling-house was surrounded by quarters where the vassals lived. So extravagant did some of the samurai become that in the *Genroku* era (1683-1703) it was found necessary to restrict the size and form of the mansions, and to prescribe different types of gate according to the rank and income. The dwelling-houses of the common people of Edo were thatched at first, but repeated fires brought about the use of tiles on the roofs in the early part of the eighteenth century, and buildings like godowns with thick mud walls became the fashion. *Cha-no-yu* continued to be in vogue, developing many " schools," but hardly anything striking in the way of architecture was in evidence.

VI.—Period of Western Influence.

Following the restoration of 1868, Western culture was eagerly sought. People went so far, at one time, as to try to destroy every institution which had no counterpart in the civilised West. Western institutions were introduced, and with them men to operate them. These included architects who taught the people how to build in brick, iron and stone after the Western style. Many school and government buildings, railway stations, modern factories, office buildings, theatres and department stores were built in the Western style. It became the fashion among the wealthy to possess a European-style house and among the middle class to furnish at least one room in European style for the reception of guests. The great earthquake and fire of 1923 proved a catastrophe to many of these foreign-style buildings, and hastened the evolution and development of special styles suited for an earthquake country like Japan.

VII.—Present : Third Nationalisation.

A reaction was inevitable. Especially since Japan's secession from the League of Nations, the national spirit has begun to reassert itself in all directions. Already its influence is being felt on architecture, designers reproducing buildings in traditional forms in reinforced concrete, and otherwise trying to reveal the native characteristics of the people while meeting the advanced requirements of the age.

HISTORIC JAPANESE BUILDINGS

This section shows the appearance of temples and palaces in Japan, which though less applicable to Western aims than purely domestic work, are important as the most elaborate type of architecture produced by the country and as the precursors of domestic style.

KONDŌ OF THE HORYUJI MONASTERY

Kondō of the Hōryuji monastery, dating from the beginning of the seventh century. This is the oldest wooden building in Japan. The gate, partly visible on the right, is also one of the original buildings, which show the excellence and lasting quality of traditional construction.

NISHI HONGWANJI TEMPLE, KYOTO

Examples of roof structure of enormous
area and weight but great simplicity.

HIGASHI HONGWANJI, NAGOYA

One of the oldest examples of a gable end, (of what was then a dwelling-house) dating from the seventh century. The building is now used as a temple. Dempōdō, Horyuji.

Three - storied pagoda of Kutaiji Temple, near Nara, overlooking a lotus pond. The pagoda has stood on the present site ever since it was removed there from Kyoto in 1135; scheduled as "National Treasure." The setting among trees is to be noted.

PAGODA OF THE KŌFUKUJI TEMPLE, NARA

Five storied pagoda of the Kōfukuji temple, Nara. The temple itself dates from the eighth century, and the present pagoda from the end of the fourteenth century. A wooden structure, with bronze bells at four corners and a bronze spire with nine rings of the same metal. The adjacent building is the Tōkondō (East Sanctuary), built at the same time as the pagoda.

GOLDEN PAVILION, KINKAKUJI TEMPLE, KYOTO

Golden Pavilion, surmounted by a gilded phœnix;
Kinkakuji Temple, Kyoto, fourteenth century. A
building famous in Japanese art.

Five - storied pagoda in Uyeno Park, Tokyo, of wood painted red, with dark grey tiled roofs. Bronze wind bells hang at four corners, and a bronze spire at the top. It stands among cherry-trees and looks beautiful when the trees bloom. The pagoda has a shaft or pillar standing on a rock in the centre and reaching to the top. In a similar pagoda at Nikko the shaft is hung from the top roof, holding the whole building together by its weight.

THE NINNAJI TEMPLE, KYOTO

Ninnaji Temple, Kyoto, showing a corner of a
building, surrounded by narrow verandah with
railings. Beyond the fence may be seen gate for the
Imperial messenger. The building shows Buddhist
influence simplified by the Japanese tradition.

INTERIOR OF THE NINNAJI TEMPLE, KYOTO

Interior of the Ninnaji Temple, Kyoto. The
Prince's room, having a slightly raised floor. In
spite of the ceremonial nature of the building the
interior shows that dignified simplicity which is
characteristic also of the dwelling-house.

SHINTO SHRINES

Shinto shrines in the primitive style of architecture, of which that of Ise is the most representative. The shrine of Ise is rebuilt every twenty years exactly in the same style, even to the minutest detail, thus keeping alive the tradition of indigenous architecture.

Nagoya Castle, the building seen on the left being the keep, a monument to the science of feudal times. The keep is surmounted by a pair of dolphins covered with sheets of gold. One of the pair was sent to the Vienna Exhibition in 1873, and recovered from the wrecked ship after remaining under water for some months. An example of Japanese ability to build solid as well as flimsy structures.

Entrance to the former detached Imperial Palace in the compound of Nagoya castle, the keep of which is seen in the background. Note the exquisite curvature of the roofs of the former Palace buildings, which were brought here and reconstructed from Hideyoshi's Palace at Momoyama. The peculiar setting of the blue granite stonework ensures safety in case of earthquake. The buildings have blue glazed tiles and whitewashed gable ends and walls.

Hikone Castle, overlooking Lake Biwa ; dating from the seventeenth century. It was the illustrious Emperor Meiji who, in spite of his progressive ideas, forbade the proposed destruction of this castle, and taught the people to have reverence for things old.

FEUDAL CASTLE, IMPERIAL PALACE GROUNDS

What remains of the feudal castle in the Imperial Palace ground, surrounded by the old moat. The curve of the granite wall as it sweeps upward gives an impression of stability. The roof's curves generally harmonise with the fir trees which overhang the moat. It is a valuable illustration of Japanese ideas of construction when applied to stone.

Opposite: (*a*) The gate for the Emperor at the Imperial Palace in Kyoto; the roof is covered with bark of *chamæcyparis obtusa* and a ridge of tile. The use of five white lines on the plastered wall is reserved for the Imperial family, princes of the blood, and temples connected with the Imperial family. The removable wooden fence is placed in front of the gate when not in use.

(*b*) An old wall, remnant of feudal Japan, now serving as the front wall of the Department of Foreign Affairs, Tokyo. Old mansions of feudal lords are fast disappearing, but a remnant, such as this, gives an interesting touch to the modern city.

GATE OF THE EMPEROR, KYOTO

WALL OF OLD FEUDAL MANSION, TOKYO

TEMPLE GATEHOUSE

OLD GATE

IMPERIAL PALACE, HAMA, TOKYO

Opposite : (*a*) A typical two-storey temple gate-house and thick mud-walls. Note the five white lines on the plastered surface of the wall. Such lines were allowed only for temples directly connected with the Imperial household, or to Imperial palaces and mansions of princes. (*b*) An old gate and a glimpse of that part of the main house where an outlet for the smoke over the kitchen may be obtained. The walls with tiled roofs are typically Japanese.

Horizontal lines suggested by water are emphasized by the horizontal effect of this group of buildings. This is part of the Imperial Palace, but there is no sense here of the superiority of man over nature.

Photo. by courtesy of the Imperial Household Department.

GATE OF THE IMPERIAL PALACE, KYOTO

GATE FOR THE IMPERIAL MESSENGER, MYOSHINJI TEMPLE, KYOTO

Each of the principal temples throughout Japan is provided with such a gate, which is kept closed and opened only for special occasions. The special gates are generally of the same type, with curved roof covered with the bark of *chamæcyparis obtusa*, as in that below. Above : the two wings with roofs protect the doors against rain while open.

44

GENERAL OBSERVATIONS

The architecture of Japan is of the lintel or trabeated (not arch) system, which throws the structural weight on pillars, the walls serving mainly as enclosures and partitions. This enables us to make large openings or windows without materially weakening the structure. The main building material is wood, there being an abundant supply of such excellent timber as *hinoki* (*chamæcyparis obtusa*), *sawara* (*chamæcyparis prisifera*), *tsuga* (hemlock), *sugi* (*cryptomeria*), *matsu* (pine), and *keyaki* (*zelkowa serrata*) in Japan. Some of this wood still remains in excellent condition on buildings of 1200-1300 years old. Statistics show that even now the greater part of the entire area of Japan is covered with forests, and there are reasons to believe that the country was almost entirely covered with primeval forests in ancient times. It was natural, therefore, for the inhabitants to build of wood. In an earthquake country like Japan this was a great boon, for no other material could have so minimised the danger resulting from earthquakes. This abundance of timber supply and the national characteristics of cleanliness and simplicity have determined and guided the general tendency of Japanese architecture.

The roof plays a part of such great importance in Japanese architecture that it is often said that the beauty of Japanese houses is in their roofs, which present a pleasing combination of straight and curved lines. There are to be found the following general types of roof : *kirizuma* (gable roof); *shichū* or *yosemune* (in which the roof slopes in four directions from the ridge pole without forming gables); *irimoya* (a roof consisting of two sections : the upper with gables as in the *kirizuma* and the lower with surfaces sloping all around the building as in the *shichū*), *hōgyō* (a roof sloping in four or more directions from a vertex without the ridge pole). These roofs are covered with thatch (straw or reeds), shingles, sheet-bronze, the bark of *hinoki*, or tiles, according to the nature of the buildings to be roofed. Generally speaking, the thatch, or thatch and tile combined, is used for farmhouses, shingles for *chaseki* (structure containing a room for *cha-no-yu*, the ceremonial tea), sheet-bronze and bark of *hinoki* for palaces and shrines, tiles for temples and ordinary dwelling houses. The beauty of these roofs consists mainly in their pleasing proportions, the curves on their surface called *teri* (suggesting a sheen) and in the eaves lines called *sori* (or curvature). These curves show Chinese influence but greatly modified, having been made much more subtle and refined.

Projecting eaves are another feature of Japanese houses. They add grace to the roof and give a sense of stability to the house. Not only from an artistic standpoint, but also from necessity have these eaves been developed. Such eaves were necessary to protect a house against heat and rain, and to allow it to be kept open on rainy days. Furthermore, in our latitude, eaves do not prevent the sun from shining into the house in the winter.

Another special feature in Japanese architecture may be found in the *masu* and *hijiki*, the brackets for supporting the eaves, which are now practically confined to religious structures. This peculiar form of bracketing was originally imported from China as a structural element above the pillars and beams, but it has been modified to serve mainly as a decorative detail.

Another pecularity may be found in the colouring. Primarily Japanese buildings were not painted; the wood was left plain, the natural colours of the different species harmonized beautifully. The colouring on Buddhist temples, which still retain traces of Chinese influence, has become much more subdued in tone. The Japanese people have special appreciation for the natural grain of wood, its texture and colour. They delight in the exquisite finish on woodwork. Carpenters work like skilled joiners in building houses, great care and skill being exercised in planing the boards for the ceiling, for instance. Often an expert planer will spend a whole day working on a few boards six feet long and one and one-half feet wide, giving an exquisitely soft sheen to the surface merely by planing. No one would ever think of soiling such a surface with paint. Paint is considered useful in covering up inferior wood or hiding defects in workmanship.

This attitude toward the plain surface of wood is a manifestation of the love of nature so strong in the Japanese. It reveals a phase of our national characteristic, which is the keynote of our architecture. Perhaps it is well for us to elaborate this point a little further. The cleanliness of our people, which we have already mentioned, cannot be over-emphasized. Even a common labourer cannot take his night's rest without his daily bath, which is easily accessible to everyone in cities as well as in rural districts. Love of nature and cleanliness, combined with a refined taste for subtle beauty, are evident in all the phases of Japanese architecture. The people are fond of the pale green of the *tatami* (wadded mats covering the floor), the texture of the natural wood in pillars and beams, the subdued colours of the plastered walls, generally of fine sand, the elegant designs on the sliding screens (*fusuma*), and the beautiful grain of the wood with the soft sheen on the ceiling. All these, mellowed by the light passing through the white paper sliding screens (*shoji*), create an exquisite atmosphere. The people have a subtle and delicate taste, refined and subdued, rather than coarse and glaring. They are of light and joyous nature, rather than pensive and vigorous. Their innate taste may be summed up in the word *shibumi*, which is difficult to translate, but whose meaning may be suggested by saying that it stands for quiet, delicate and refined taste, the beauty that does not show on the surface, austerity in art without severity; and that it is opposed to anything which is gaudy, crude or ostentatious. Without *shibumi* (literally astringency) no art can be worth while, no person worth knowing, and no house worth inhabiting.

The religious ideas of the people have, of course, been a great factor in influencing the trend of Japanese architecture. Shintoism, the inherent faith based on nature and ancestor-worship, and Buddhism, which was imported from Korea and China, have both gone far in shaping and developing Japanese architecture, the former insisting on simplicity and the latter showing a tendency to the ornate. These two opposing elements have been struggling against each other. The result seems to prove the strength of the innate taste for simplicity as shown by the fact that some of the Shinto shrines still retain their original simplicity, while Buddhist temples show marked traces of having been simplified in many respects. Simplicity is the keynote of Japanese dwelling-houses, as may be gathered from our illustrations.

In the Far East, where the family is the unit of society, the home assumes a position of prime importance in the life of the people, and it is but natural that the house should have received the most careful attention in various ways. The health and prosperity of a person were considered to depend on the location and planning of the dwelling-house chiefly in reference to " direction." With due consideration given to the various necessary elements for making the house pleasant and hygienic, the following rules have come to be regarded as the standard to be followed : an ideal site for a house should have a stream on the left (east) and a long road on the right (west), a pond in front (south) and hills at the back (north). According to the ancient Chinese astrologers and physiographers, the stream represents " green dragon," the road " white tiger," the pond " Shujaku " (a sort of phœnix), and the hills " genbu " (delineated in art by a turtle entwined with a snake), the four symbols representing the Buddhist deities safeguarding the four directions. The principle involved is the same as that which governs the growth of all living things in the universe. It is the principle of the positive and negative, of male and female, or of sunshine and shadow, in which one mingles harmoniously with the other. Another ancient book has it that it is lucky for a man to live in a house built on ground which rises at the back and slopes down in front ; woe unto the person who dwells in a house standing on ground with a rise in the front and a downward slope at the back. In these statements it is presumed that the house faces the south, whence comes sunshine and good cheer. On ground which is low, and open both to the east and to the south and high on the west and north, the house may face east, south-east or south and still have rising ground at the back and is hence desirable. However, should a building be facing west or north and have hills at the back, then the sunshine and warmth from the east or south would be shut off, and the location be undesirable. It also states that great prosperity will attend a house built on a plateau surrounded by rising hills, but misfortune will haunt the house situated at the top of a height which slopes down on all sides to a plain. According to this belief there should be a hill or big trees at the back of the house where the " spirit " of the atmosphere may hover about and safely nestle.

The plan of the house, of course, depends on the location, but it should have due regard to " direction " determined by imaginary lines drawn from the north-east to the south-west, and from the north-west to the south-east, intersecting each other at right angles at the heart of the house. The north-east is called " ki-mon " (devil's gate) and care should be taken not to build anything unclean in that direction. Undesirable things are said to come from that direction and the house should be so planned as to be protected by a wall or a closet in that direction and not be left open. The south-east is designated as the " chi-mon " (earth's gate) or " fū-mon " (wind's gate), the north-west as the " ten-mon " (heaven's gate) where the well and the store-house should be located, and the south-west, between the heaven and earth gates, as the " jin-mon " (man's gate). These " directions," though some are inclined to disregard them as being mere superstition, seem to be based mainly on hygienic principles and on atmospheric conditions such as the direction of the prevailing winds or storms. Such importance is attached in the mind of the people to these rules that it is still customary in Japan to consult a specialist on "directions " when one wishes to build a home. Again, when there is frequent sickness in the house one will often go to him to have the " physiognomy " of the house examined, and to make necessary alterations to conform to these laws.

One outstanding feature in Japanese architecture is the existence of a convenient unit—the *ken*—which equals 6 ft. and serves as the basis of measurement. Some scholars trace the origin of the *ken* to the beginning of the eighth century, when the capital of the Empire was established at Nara with perfectly regular streets parallel and at right angles like the lines on a checkerboard. However that may be, it is clear that early in history a *ken* (or *ma*) designated the distance between two pillars in a building, though the distance varied. But with various modifications, it came to represent a fixed measurement in the second half of the fifteenth century when *tatami* (wadded mats) came to be in common use. Strictly speaking there are four regulation sizes of the *tatami* with slight variations : length 7 ft., width 3.5 ft., thickness 4 inches for rooms in a palace ; length 6.6 ft., width 3.3 ft., thickness $2\frac{1}{4}$ in. for the " Kōya-ma " (rooms of the Kōya temples) ; length 6.3 ft., width 3.15 ft., thickness $2\frac{1}{8}$ in. for " Kyō-ma " (rooms of Kyoto houses), and length 5.8 ft., width 2.9 ft., thickness $1\frac{1}{8}$ in. for " Edo-ma " (rooms in Tokyo houses). But commonly for dwelling-houses either the " Kyō-ma " or " Edo-ma " size is used, generally speaking the " Kyō-ma " size prevailing in the western part of Japan, and the " Edo-ma " in the eastern part. The difference in the two standards arises chiefly from the fact that the *ken* unit is applied in the former to the distance between the pillars, while in the latter the measurement is taken from centre to centre of the pillars. In fact, in the Kyō-ma the size of the *tatami* is fixed and uniform and the rooms are built to accommodate an exact number of mats, the mats thus being interchangeable with those of other rooms, while in the Edo-ma the *tatami* are made to fit each particular room exactly, there being a very slight variation in dimensions, but each measuring about 6 ft., by 3 ft., roughly speaking. The size of the room is expressed by the number of mats covering its floor space completely, the common sizes of rooms requiring $4\frac{1}{2}$, 6, 8, 10, 12 and $12\frac{1}{2}$ mats respectively. Two mats laid alongside forming a 6-foot square, is 1 *tsubo*, which is the unit of measurement for surface.

Such being the case, the log or lumber is furnished in 1, $1\frac{1}{2}$, 2, $2\frac{1}{2}$ *ken* and so on, with a certain additional length in each case to allow for the dressing. This simplifies matters very much, and helps to economise the material considerably. When one is building a house the time-honoured custom is to get suitable material in logs and have the sawyer saw it up according to requirements, the carpenter marking them to get the best out of them. In marking, as well as in utilizing the lumber, the carpenters always bear in mind what they call the " back " and the " belly " of the tree. In the case of trees growing on level ground the sunny side with thriving branches is called the " back," while the shady side where the development is not so good is called the " belly "; but in the case of trees growing on a steep hillside the side exposed to the open space is the " back " and the reverse which faces the up-slope of the hill is the " belly." The logs should be sawed from the " belly " to the " back," as this minimises waste of material and energy and the lumber so made is stronger. Carpenters also bear in mind that each piece of lumber has a topside and an underside, the former being the side near the bark, and the latter close to the core—the outer concentric arcs of the grain being the topside and the inner arcs the underside. As the board warps towards the topside with the tendency of the grain to be in straight lines, the lumber should be used with the topside up in flooring, roofing and so forth. For *shikii* (the grooved piece on the floor between two posts) and *kamoi* (the grooved upper beam) the grooves should be made on the topside so that the partitions will slide back and forth more smoothly. When planing the topside of the lumber it should be planed from the end of the tree toward its root, and the process should be reversed when dealing with the underside. Otherwise one would be planing against the grain of the wood. Though the underside is softer and easier for the carpenter to plane than the topside, it often leaves bristles on the surface, so the topside is generally chosen to secure a hard, smooth surface. However, for special purposes, such as the clap boards on the outside of the house, the underside is planed and exposed, as it is easier to plane and there are fewer knots on it and it is better suited for preservation. As it is not possible always to get perfectly seasoned lumber, Japanese carpenters usually guard themselves against mischief done by shrinkage. Square and round timbers for pillars, if they are so used as to have one side hidden from view, are split open on that side as far as the centre and wedges inserted so that the exposed parts may preserve their shape and surface free from warping and cracking.

The necessities of construction and a fine sense of proportion have established a certain standard in the construction of the Japanese house. For instance, in the ordinary middle-class house the standard measurements are as follows : 2.2 ft. from the bottom of the beam resting on the foundation stones to the top of the *tatami*, 5.8 ft. from the floor groove level with the *tatami* to the upper groove, on the underside of the beam, which is about 2 in. high under the *uchinori nageshi* of 4.5 in. in height. Then comes the narrow upper wall, with or without *ramma* (sliding screens or openwork carvings for ornament and ventilation), of 3.4 ft., and over it the *tenjō* (ceiling) *nageshi* $3\frac{3}{8}$ in. high, topped by the *tenjō mawari buchi* of $2\frac{3}{4}$ in. high, upon which rests the ceiling, generally of boards less than half an inch thick. The height of the ceiling from the matted floor is slightly over 10 ft. The standard size of the sliding partitions, which separate one room from another or from the corridor, and which may be removed in order to throw several rooms into one big hall, is 5.8 ft. by 3 ft., though the partition between pillars, 9, 15 or sometimes 12 ft., apart is generally made in four screens, the width of the screens varying.

In order to get pleasing proportions the size of the pillar is determined by its length and by the dimensions of the room in which it is used. In ordinary dwelling-houses the pillar is made $4\frac{1}{2}$ in. square if it is 9 ft. in length ; $4\frac{3}{4}$ in. square for 11 ft. ; 5 in. square for 12 ft. ; $5\frac{1}{4}$ in. square for 13 ft. ; $5\frac{1}{2}$ in. square for 14 ft. ; $5\frac{3}{4}$ in. square for 15 ft. ; 6 in. square for 16 ft. ; and $6\frac{1}{4}$ in. square for 17 ft. The size of the pillar becomes the standard for all the other parts, such as the foundation beams, which should be 10 per cent. larger, the lower grooves to be of equal width, the upper grooved beam to be 90 per cent. for the width and 35-40 per cent. for the height, the lower *nageshi* to be 80-95 per cent. for the height and the upper *nageshi* from 60 to 65 per cent. of the dimension of the pillar for the height.

The *tokonoma* (a recess in the main room for paintings and other ornaments) is an important feature in the Japanese home and perhaps more than any other part is its construction governed by established proportion. It is generally 1 or $1\frac{1}{2}$ *ken* (6 or 9 ft) in length and one-half or a quarter of a *ken* in depth in ordinary-sized rooms. It is the place of honour, and the matting in front of it is always reserved for guests. Adjoining it is usually another recess called the *toko-waki* (*tokonoma*-side) with *chigai-dana* (shelves of uneven length on different levels) and small cupboards with sliding doors ; and the pillar dividing the two recesses or alcoves called the *toko-bashira*, is the most important pillar in the house. Its size is taken as the standard in determining the size of the front piece (*toko-kamachi*), to the level of which the floor of the *tokonoma* is raised, the size of the beam (*otoshigake*) supporting the narrow overhanging wall across the top front of the *tokonoma*, and the position of that beam in reference to the *nageshi* supporting the overhanging wall in front of the *toko-waki*. The proportions used in the construction of the *tokonoma* and the sizes and shapes of the shelves and closets in the *toko-waki* are always considered very carefully.

It may be well to add here that a commission was organized in June 1919, by the Japanese Government to investigate the unification of weights and measures as well as engineering standards, and that this body decided on the adoption of the metric system as the standard in Japan. Prior to this time engineering standardisation was first established in Japan in 1905 in testing methods of Portland cement ; the Japanese Electro-Technical Committee has been engaged since 1910 in the work of standardising the nomenclature, rating, etc., of electrical machinery and instruments ; and the Water Supply Association drew up in 1913 the standard specifications for cast-iron water-pipes. After the special commission had decided on the adoption of the metric system for the country, the Japanese Engineering Standard Committee was established in 1921, and is divided into the following four sections : metals, non-metallic materials, electrical machinery and instruments, and mechanical equipments and supplies. These sections have thirty-one subcommittees in all. So far nearly one hundred standards have been approved in Japan, but what I have referred to in these notes as the common rules of practice in Japanese architecture, have nothing to do with the work of the Standards Committee mentioned above. Japan formally adopted the metric system a few years ago, yet it will take some time before the general public becomes familiar with the new system. Whatever the system of measurement, the common rules formulated by centuries of practice in architecture and with intimate knowledge of woods will remain substantially unchanged for ages to come.

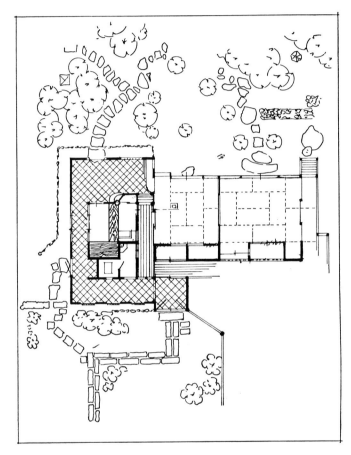

A plan of a modern Japanese house, showing its relation to the garden. Part of the floor space is tiled (shown by crossed lines) and part occupied by the traditional tatami. From each door stepping-stones lead into the garden. To the bottom right a sleeve fence is seen projecting from the verandah.

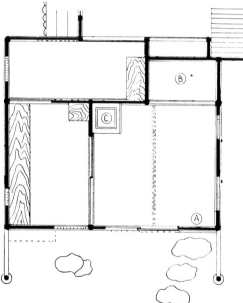

Right : Plan of a typical modern chaseki. *(A) shows the crawling-in entrance, approached by stepping-stones, (B) the tokonoma, and (C) the charcoal brazier sunk in the floor.*

THE JAPANESE HOUSE TO-DAY

The Japanese house, built in the traditional style, is in a way much more fragile than one constructed in the Western style, though it is able to meet all requirements, both natural and human, just as well if not better. It is generally made to stand on small foundation-stones, one stone for each underpinning. The structure is not connected with the ground, but is weighed down mainly by the tiles on the roof. The houses are thus top-heavy, but because of the weight of the roof the structure is able to withstand strong winds. The walls, too, add weight, for they are of mud and finished with fine sand or plaster on the surface. Mud is used also on the roof to keep the tiles in position, although they are further secured by means of wire.

What Japanese carpenters do seems often directly opposite to what Western carpenters would do under similar circumstances. Some of their tools are made to be used differently. Take for instance the saw ; the Japanese saw is so shaped and toothed as to cut when it is drawn toward oneself, instead of when it is pushed away. The plane, too, is so made that it shaves the surface when the tool is pulled, instead of when it is forced away.

Similarly a reverse order may be found in the construction of a house. Japanese carpenters usually employ logs, or bent trees in their natural form, for the tie-beams that hold the roof together, the part that serves as the main structure of the roof. It is customary for the carpenters to construct the roof framework first on the ground, though provisionally, every piece properly fitted and held by tenons, or by wedges, but not nailed. Then it is pulled apart and put aside for the time being. They proceed to prepare other pieces of timber, cutting mortises and tenons and fitting them together ; each piece being numbered and marked before being pulled apart. The posts and beams which are to be exposed to the room or corridors when finished are completely covered with paper and thin glue in order to protect the surface. When all the essential members are ready the framework of the house, if it is not too large, is generally put up in a single day, a significant occasion in the construction of the house, called the *mune-age*, a term signifying the raising of the ridge-pole to its place, thus completing the framework of the house. Generally the occasion is celebrated with a ceremony and feast.

Usually the underpinnings are a few inches above two feet, each resting on a stone, the usual height of the floor being about 2 ft. 7 in. to 3 ft. above the ground. Dovetailing and the mortise and tenon joints are used extensively, but nails also are freely used to hold members together. Pieces of split bamboo are generally used for laths, these pieces being wound and fastened together with straw rope, and mud mixed with short rice straw for binding is plastered on, making solid mud walls of some 4 or 5 in. thick. The first wall requires to be thoroughly dried before the second coating is applied on top of it. For finishing the surface of the wall, certain kinds of clay or fine sands of one shade or another are commonly used. The sands are mixed with a size prepared from seaweeds, which remains effective for a number of years. White lime plaster is also employed for the top coating, it being more durable, though less artistic in appearance. Hardly any wall paper is in evidence.

The floor of the dwelling house is boarded and then completely covered with *tatami*, wadded mats. At the time of the general house-cleaning, these mats can be taken out and sunned, the floor-board taken up and the ground under the floor swept. No room has a cement or earthen floor, except the old-fashioned kitchen, which is fast disappearing.

The ceiling consists generally of boards, usually 1 ft. 2 in. or 1 ft. 5 in. wide and 6 ft. long, held on the underside with narrow pieces of wood placed parallel to each other about 1 ft. 5 in. apart and at right angles to the board. On to these narrow strips the ceiling boards, which are about $\frac{3}{8}$ in. thick, are nailed from the topside so that no nail is visible in the room. The whole ceiling is suspended by means of strips of wood nailed to beams not visible from the room. Great care is exercised in choosing these boards for the ceiling. Boards cut from the same piece of timber, or of similar grains are chosen for the ceiling of the entire room. The grains of the wood should be consistent as far as the room is concerned; using one kind of wood, of a uniform size, and of similar grains; thus if the grain is wavy, the same general pattern of grain should be followed throughout, and if straight, other patterns should not be introduced. For this reason, people often buy a big log and have the sawyer cut from it as necessary. The ceiling of one room is often made different from that of another in the house so that there may be a variation. A favourite wood for this purpose is cryptomeria. Some of the boards with rare grains are extremely costly, though nowadays veneered boards have come to the rescue. Not only the ceiling, but the whole woodwork of a room or suite of rooms—beams, posts and all—is often carried out in one particular kind of wood. The woodwork is hardly ever stained or coloured.

Houses are usually built to face the south; that is, they are open to the south. There should be enough opening on the northern side also to permit a current of air to pass through from north to south and *vice versa*; this gives warmth in winter and coolness in summer. Comparatively few walls are constructed; wherever possible sliding screens are employed, to move between the upper and lower grooves of two beams. These screens can be easily removed from the grooves, and this enables the house to be converted into one large room when occasion requires, to accommodate large crowds of people together. These sliding screens may be one of the following three kinds : *fusuma* (panels made by covering a wooden framework with decorated paper on both sides), *shoji* (wooden frame covered on one side only with plain white paper so as to admit light) or *sugito* (wooden panelled doors with or without decorations). By careful use the *fusuma* may not require remounting for a number of years, but the *shoji* should have fresh papering at least once a year, as the paper gets brownish and untidy. These screens may be put away during summer months and replaced by *misu* (a sort of curtain made of split bamboo or reeds) which are hung from the beam, or by sliding screens made of reeds which allow the draught to go through and give a cool effect.

The most important feature in the interior of the Japanese house is the *tokonoma*, the alcove for ornaments, a room with such an alcove being known as *shoin-zukuri*, suggesting a sort of study. Ordinarily this alcove is 3 ft. deep and 6 or 9 ft. wide, the back wall serving for hanging scrolls of painting or writing, generally one, sometimes a pair, and rarely a set of three at a time. The floor of it is used for a vase or basket of flowers, or a small stand with an incense burner, or for both. The alcove is regarded with reverence, and no one would step on it without a good excuse. If one is a guest in the house one should first obtain permission from the host to do so when one wishes to examine the painting more closely. The space adjoining the *tokonoma* on the side is generally used for shelves and cupboards fixed to the wall to serve also for ornaments, these being known as *chigai-dana*, which signifies shelves of uneven height and length. The cupboard is often constructed along the ceiling above the shelves, or on the floor below them, or often both. Thus one end of the room is entirely taken up by *tokonoma* and *chigai-dana*. The greatest care is taken in the construction of these features, which are usually confined to the guest room or reception room, but are made in other rooms as well. The post between the *tokonoma* and *chigai-dana* has always been considered very important in the Japanese house. It marks the most honoured place in the room ; the guest of the highest honour will sit in front of it. For that post rare wood is often used. The beam that supports the narrow curtain wall hanging from the ceiling in front of the *tokonoma*, as well as the border on the floor, marking the front and the *chigai-dana* side of the *tokonoma*, are next in importance. The former is generally plain, while the latter is often lacquered black or transparent reddish-brown, allowing the grain of the wood to show through. The floor of the alcove, which is usually covered with matting, is made flush with the top of the border pieces, and three to four inches higher than the floor of the room. The floor of the space where the shelves are constructed is generally of one piece of wood, finely grained, the level of the board being the same as that of the *tatami* in the room. Beautiful grains of wood are much in evidence in the woodwork.

The *genkan*, the front entrance, is another feature of the Japanese house. It generally provides for a sheltered extension, into which vehicles may be drawn. It is convenient to have such a protection because of the necessity for everybody to remove their shoes or whatever footgear they may be wearing before entering the house, a custom still followed very closely even in dwelling-houses of European style in Japan. There are house slippers for the corridors, which are left outside the room when entering it. The removing of the shoes worn outside before entering the house is not only a hygienic custom long in practice in Japan, but is almost imperative because of the muddy roads and streets, and also of the nature of the floor covering. The custom of kneeling on the floor, and the cleanly habits of the people further support the custom of refusing to allow outside dirt to be carried into the house. The *genkan* is a decorative adjunct to the house ; it gives a dignity and an artistic touch where it is most needed. Sometimes in the feudal regime it was thought to be too extravagant for the dwelling-houses of the common people, and the use of it was prohibited. But such a law was in force only for a short duration, and the feature was developed as an integral part of the Japanese dwelling-house.

The close relation existing between the house and the garden should not be overlooked when considering Japanese dwelling-houses. For many centuries the Japanese house was developed as a part of the garden whenever the premises were large enough. No house is considered complete without a garden of some sort, and the garden is almost an integral part of the house. A stone water-basin installed close to the house serves as an ornament in the garden and can be used from the verandah for washing one's hands. It generally has a short fence known as " sleeve-fence " built out from the house a few feet into the garden, partly as an ornament and partly to obstruct the view of another part from the verandah. This, too, serves to connect the house with the garden. Large natural stones are placed close to the verandah to be used as steps leading into the garden, and are followed by a number of stepping-stones. All these bind the house and the garden into an inseparable whole. Trees should be planted close enough to the house to have their shadows silhouetted on the paper sliding screens in the house. By pushing these screens to one side, or removing them altogether, the entire room is thrown open to the garden, thereby satisfying the strong desire of the people living in these houses to be close to nature even while in the house.

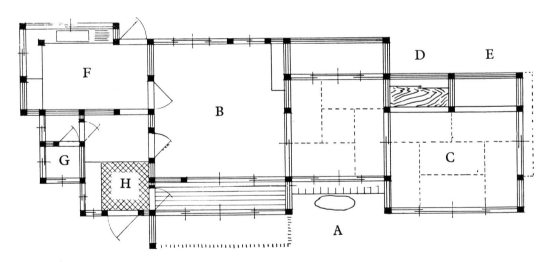

Plan of a modern Japanese house. A. front entrance with stepping-stone ; B. main room, containing chairs ; C. guest room ; D. toko-waki and E. tokonoma (both within C) ; F. kitchen ; G. w.c. ; H. bathroom. Note the verandah to the left of the entrance.

The shinden-zukuri *style of architecture, developed by the wealthy aristocracy of the tenth century, from which the style of the present day has developed. This is a nobleman's country seat, consisting of rectangular buildings joined by long corridors to make three sides of a square, and enclosing a landscape garden of which the main feature is a lake with an island in it, reached by ornamental bridges.*

THE EXTERIOR

*In simplicity and in harmony, deliberately contrived between
the structure and its surroundings, so that it becomes a part of
the landscape, the exterior of the Japanese house offers many
suggestions to the West.*

The Shōsōin, the Imperial repository, dating from A.D. 752 is built of wood, and divided into three
sections. The staircase and verandah are temporary during the annual " airing " of treasures. It
is in the *azegura* style of architecture peculiar to store-houses of the eighth century. The outer
walls are formed by laying triangular timbers horizontally, crossing at the corners. The theory is
that the least moisture in the air will expand the wood and shut the moisture out, and the dryness
will cause the air to circulate freely, thus keeping the treasures within free from mildew.

THE SHŌSŌIN-SUPPORTING PILLARS

The Shōsōin is supported by forty massive pillars, resting on stones and raising the floor about nine feet above the ground. This may counter the impression that Japanese buildings are flimsy. This construction has stood for many years without other treatment than proper seasoning of the wood in the first place.

Detail showing how triangular timbers are crossed at the corner on the building of the Shōsōin, an eighth-century Imperial repository at Nara, where it still stands. Some parts show an erosion of about two and half inches, the wood having been eaten away by wind, rain and exposure during twelve centuries.

COTTAGE IN A GARDEN AT NARA

A cottage in Mr. Seki's garden at Nara.
The cottage is called " Sanschu-tei " which
indicates that from it one can enjoy three
surpassing views of mountain peaks famous
in literature.

PAVILION IN MARQUIS ASANO'S GARDEN

Pavilion in Marquis Asano's garden named " Sentei," the name suggesting that it is essentially of water. The garden has the famous stone arching bridge across the pond, and a temporary bridge along the side of it now prevents the arch from forming a circle with its reflection on the water. The pavilion with its generous eaves has the virtue of being unobtrusive.

THATCHED HOUSE, HAKKEI-YEN, HIKONE

Thatched house built over a pond in the garden. The evergreens form the architecture of the garden, being more or less permanent features. Note shrubs on left, protected against cold winds and frosts.

A two-roomed cottage in Nara Park, the thatched roof with a pottery basin inverted at the top. Full advantage has been taken of the variation of levels to give picturesqueness of appearance.

A CHASEKI UNDER SNOW

A *chaseki* under snow. The charm of its outward aspect is in keeping with the æsthetic joy one may feel in the boiling kettle and when sipping the green beverage out of a black raku bowl.

The south side of Mrs. Majima's home at Kamakura. It is essential to have the south side of the house open for warmth in winter and coolness in summer. The long fixed bench, about two feet in depth, is called an *en* or *en-gawa* in Japanese. When it is outside sliding doors, as in this case, it is called *nure-en*, or wet *en*.

Sometimes the house is so built as to have its floor four or five feet above the ground, in order to safeguard the house against damp. The space below the floor is protected by a screen of bars and nets constructed under the verandah to keep dogs and cats out.

A tile-roofed two-storied private home at Kyoto, entirely open toward the garden on the south side, whence come light and warmth. Houses, whether large or small, all have regard to the natural appearance of their gardens.

APPROACH TO THE HOUSE OF MR. YAGI, KYOTO

Approach to the main entrance of Mr. Yagi's home at Kyoto. There is an " island," constructed with rocks and trees in front of it so as not to expose the entrance too plainly, and flanking a carriage drive. This is typical of a wealthy person's house.

The Japanese house generally has two entrances : *omote genkan*, the main entrance for the guests, and *nai-genkan*, the side entrance for the family.

The entrance to the house at the right, and
to the garden at the left ; round windows
with sliding glass doors.

The curvature of the roof over the front steps shows the style which was in vogue in the Tokugawa régime.

HOUSE AT ATAMI, IZU PROVINCE

A house built of wood on a steep slope; with roof covered with painted sheet-iron.

The roof of a koshikake covered with cryptomeria-wood bark and dressed with bamboo. The roof is literally tied together.

ENTRANCE TO THE HOME OF MRS. MAJIMA, KAMAKURA

Entrance to the home of Mrs. Majima, of Kamakura. It shows an interesting thatched roof with an open-ended ridge, originally an outlet for smoke. The tassel hanging at the entrance is the New Year decoration.

The thatched roofs seem to grow out of the land and to become an integral part of the landscape.

FARMER'S COTTAGE

A farmer's cottage celebrating the boys' festival which is observed on the fifth day of the fifth month of the year.

How traditional wood structure adapts itself to the hill-side. The nearest building is a restaurant ; those on the left are shops.

HOUSE OF MR. AMAMIYA

The box built at the left corner is for keeping the wooden doors (called *amado*, or rain doors), which are pulled out and pushed along the groove outside the glass doors for the night. The stone steps help to connect the garden to the house, which shows a pleasant blending of natural and artificial forms.

JAPANESE RESTAURANT, NEAR YAMAGUCHI

A water garden among buildings. Wind-swept nature is imitated in the shaping of small bushes, etc. There is a verandah from which the garden can be enjoyed.

HOUSE OF FEUDAL VASSAL, OLD SAMURAI MANSION, KAMEYAMA

HOUSE NEAR KAMEYAMA, ISE PROVINCE

The building above is of unpainted wood with grey-tiled roofs ; that below of wood and bamboo, with thick mud walls.

OLD WAREHOUSE, KAMEYAMA

THE HOUSE OF BARON KONDO, TOKYO

The group of trees on the left hand serves to conceal the house from outside, and another group further to the right hides the entrance to the kitchen. Wooden building with tiled roofs. The extension of the left side is furnished in a European style and used as a parlour.

THE HOSHIGAOKA CHARYO FROM GARDEN

A view of the Hoshigaoka Charyo from the garden. The ground is covered with pine needles for the winter. Sliding glass screens, it will be noted, replace the traditional paper screens.

VILLA ON THE BANK OF THE OKAWA RIVER, ITO, IZU PROVINCE

A broad verandah inside the glass sliding doors, and outside the rooms partitioned by paper sliding screens, has a wooden floor, where a table and chairs give comfort even to Japanese, who are accustomed to sit on the floor.

HOUSE OF MR. B. SHIRASU

The turret at the left side shows a treatment of
the chimney of the drawing-room fireplace. A
house combining Western ideas with the native
style.

HOUSE OF MR. HARA, YOKOHAMA

In perfect harmony with the wooded hills surrounding it, this building well shows the
Japanese feeling for nature.

This thatched-roofed temple seen from a bamboo grove shows the intimate connection established between building and garden.

KŌBUNTEI IN TOKIWA KŌYEN, MITO

Above : This interesting piece of construction does not take precedence over the garden. It gives full value to the trees and shrubs, though obviously their shapes have been controlled. The house was built by a feudal lord, and now belongs to the City of Mito.

Opposite : (a) Approach to the entrance of the old home of Lord Ii of feudal Japan. The clump of trees in front of the entrance obstructs the view into the house from the gate, giving the necessary privacy to the occupants. (b) A thatch-roofed *hanare* in the garden of Mr. Inahata's home in Kyoto. It is built on a hill, and is therefore well protected by tall hedges and trees.

a.

HANARE, HOUSE OF MR. INAHATA, KYOTO

b.

OKYO BUILDING, GARDEN OF BARON MASUDA, TOKYO

Okyo Building, so named because of its mural decorations painted by the famous artist, Maruyama Okyo. For many years the building stood in the garden of Baron Masuda, Tokyo, but it was recently donated to the Imperial Household Museum, in the compound of which it is to be re-erected and preserved. The " floor " of this garden is its main interest. It is not cut up into bits. The simple plane in front of the building gives great dignity and allows attention to be focused on the trees and upon the building. A good-looking building in a simple dress !

Though built on the brink of the Biwa Lake, the house is surrounded by tall trees and only from an upstairs room may a glimpse of the lake be obtained through a gap in the trees. A stream runs through the garden, which creates a world of its own.

HOUSE OF MR. ICHIDA, KYOTO

The side of the house facing the garden can be thrown entirely open in order to get the full benefit of it. The house appears as a part of the garden.

HOUSE OF MR. NODA, KYOTO

Split bamboo or reed curtains are hung outside the verandah to be cool in the house. The screen also acts as a veil : the occupants of the rooms can see outside but are protected from being seen.

With an exposed corridor with a low railing, the building is most intimately connected with the garden.
Photo. by courtesy of the Imperial Household Museum

The narrow ground between the pavement and the house is treated as a garden, which is here shown in its winter garments : the ground covered with pine needles and a cabbage plant protected with a rice-straw covering. Cabbages are cultivated by the Japanese for their decorative value.

HOUSE IN THE SHINJUKU IMPERIAL GARDEN

The house and garden have been arranged with due regard to the purpose and recognition of natural forms and colour and to the lie of the land.

The entrance to the house is generally in latticed glass sliding doors. At night wooden panelled doors (*amado*) are pulled out for a greater protection on a groove outside those of the glass doors. A simple but effective wooden grilled outer door.

IMPERIAL GARDEN OF THE AKASAKA PALACE

By courtesy of the Imperial Household Department

The building is hidden just enough by surrounding trees so as not to obtrude itself.

This was the home of a feudal lord.   The thatch-roofed houses look picturesque in the garden with its big lake.

A CHASEKI, GARDEN OF MR. HIRAI, KYOTO

A thatched roof, round and square windows. The plaque on the gable bears the name of the *chaseki* —" sei-ryo," meaning pure and cool. The stream that runs by it and the pine-tree that spreads over it, help to bring out the significance of the name. See the curve of the pine-trees' branches and how they seem to hold the roof of the house. This is a good lesson in harmony and in modesty of both builder and owner. Note the shape of the " sleeve fence."

GATEWAY, HOUSE OF MR. N. MORI, M.P., TOKYO

The gateway with tiled roof leads into the garden, which is totally enclosed by a wall.

GATEWAY AT MR. WATANABE'S VILLA, TOKYO

A garden gate, with a shingle roof and tiled ridge,
at the former home of Mr. J. Watanabe, Shitaya
Ward, Tokyo.   A view from outside.

ENTRANCE GATE, VILLA OF MR. A. SAMI, NAGAHAMA

The approach to the entrance of the house is carefully planned through the garden. This shows a wooden bridge in front of an inner gate, where a glimpse of the entrance may be obtained.

HOUSE OF MR. ICHIDA, KYOTO

Effort is generally made not to expose the house too much to the view, as in the case of Mr. Ichida's home in Kyoto here shown. By the aid of large trees it is half-concealed from whatever position in the garden one may look at it.

HALL IN KŌRAKUYEN, A PUBLIC PARK IN OKAYAMA

The public hall in Kōrakuyen, a public park in Okayama, which was originally a garden built for the people of the city by a feudal lord, whose castle still stands on the height across the river flowing close by. It shows an interesting treatment of one end of the building in thatch-roof.

PAVILION IN KIYOSUMI-YEN, FUKAGAWA, TOKYO

This pavilion in Kiyosumi-yen was built in honour of Lord Kitchener, who visited Baron Iwasaki's villa, to which the garden belonged. The garden with its buildings was later given to the city of Tokyo. Inborn fondness for beautiful natural scenes makes verandah-making second nature.

VILLA OF MR. NAKAMURA, NARA

Showing curtains made of reeds hanging from the eaves to shut off the glare of the sun in summer. A simple sleeve fence of bamboo, to obstruct the view of the room from another part of the house, may be seen built close to the house.

The building is equipped with a kitchen, a room for waiting, a bench for the intervals, as well as the room for tea. *Photo. by courtesy of the Imperial Household Museum.*

Shoes are removed before entering the house and the entrance-room (*genkan*) is so constructed as to be convenient for the custom. A *kutsunugi-ishi* (shoe-removing stone), and a step in ascending to the room in the house, are shown.

A CHASEKI IN THE GARDEN OF MRS. MAJIMA, KAMAKURA

The nearer cottage is in shingle roof, and the
further in thatch, ridges of both ornamented with
bamboo. Peace and quiet hover here, silence
being only intensified by the murmur of the
stream running close by.

A CHASEKI IN THE GARDEN OF MR. HARA, YOKOHAMA

The stepping stones lead to the small square entrance to the ceremonial tea room. The entrance is called *nijiri-guchi*, meaning one has to kneel in entering it. One is supposed to leave everything outside — shoes, hat, rank, worldly ambition, etc.—and enter as a plain man.

A CHASEKI IN THE GARDEN OF BARON SUMITOMO, KYOTO

A *chaseki* in Baron Sumitomo's garden in Kyoto.
Tranquillity dwells in it as the shimmering light,
filtered through the leaves of the trees, falls upon
it, creating interesting masses of light and
shadow. The apparently casual effect is planned
with care and labour.

A CHASEKI IN THE GARDEN OF THE IMPERIAL
HOUSEHOLD MUSEUM, TOKYO

Rokusō-an, the six-windowed *chaseki* for ceremonial tea, in the garden of the Imperial Household Museum of Tokyo. A thatch-roofed house,
surrounded by trees, with a secluded garden of its
own, the *chaseki* is full of tranquillity, a splendid
place for meditation.

The inside of the front gate, showing a small private entrance at the side, and a path paved with pebbles. The high plain wall becomes interesting with shadows of beautifully trained pine trees.

GATEWAY AT THE VILLA OF MR. NAKAMURA, NARA

A gateway of pleasing proportions at Mr. Nakamura's villa in Nara, designed and executed by M. Shimojima, of Kyoto. It is of plain woodwork, with a shingle roof and tile ridge, and is seen from inside the garden.

A thatch-roofed cottage showing a gable end. The skirts of the exterior walls are protected by covering them with split bamboo. The corner posts fit neatly upon stones hammered into the ground.

This corridor is covered with a roof of cryptomeria bark with a ridge of tiles. The pillars stand on octagonal stone bases.

This entrance, with its narrow artistic stone pavement, is famous in Japan for its masterly construction and dates from the early seventeenth century.

The sliding screens may be easily removed so as to have the room entirely open to the garden. One may sit on the small bench at the corner and lose himself in meditation even when the room is shut. The bamboo conduit fills the small pond, which has an intimate relation with the house.

WATER-BASIN

The *chōzubachi*, the basin for washing hands, has been made a feature of in Japanese houses. It has developed a formula for the arrangement of various stones about it, and necessitated an extension of the verandah for using the basin. Various designs have been adopted for this extension. Here is an example.

Chōzubachi, a water basin for washing hands, always placed near the toilet, is used from the house with a long-handled dipper. It generally accompanies a sleeve-fence (*sode-gaki*) both of which act as connecting link between the house and garden.

GARDEN GATE OF A HOUSE IN ITO, IZU PROVINCE

A garden gate and fence, partitioning the inner
from the outer garden. The fence is made of
bamboo, and what looks like straw are the
leaves of the bamboo.

The far-extending eaves give beautiful soft shadows to the house. The gateway and trees beyond the fence give depth to the garden.

Square and round windows give a variety to the rest-arbour. The round window is provided with a hook for hanging a lantern at night, and the pillars with natural bark stand on unhewn stones.

A hut on a knoll in the garden is connected with large stepping stones so as to make it easily accessible from the main house. A sort of sleeve-wall with a round window, latticed with bamboo, makes the house picturesque with its triangular gables.

A CHASEKI WITH OPEN SKYLIGHT

The *chaseki* generally has a skylight to be pushed up from inside as shown in the illustration. It is called the *tsuki-age mado*. It gives not only necessary light into the room, but also a glimpse of the trees which are generally found near by.

A room often has a garden of its own, being open to a small space of which a natural garden is made with a few stones, shrubs and grass. Thus the room and the garden together create a world in themselves.

There is peace and tranquillity in the garden of a *chaseki*, whose deep eaves cast soft shadows on the papered window, mellowing the light in the tea room and making it a fit place for quiet meditation.

Opposite : One side of the *chaseki* is often so constructed as to be opened wide. This is called the *kinin-guchi*, or entrance for the nobility. However, within the *chaseki* rank and birth are transcended.

VERANDAH

ENTRANCE TO CHASEKI

The ceiling of the verandah is of braided shingles, and the underside of the eaves shows slender rafters supported by natural pillars. The variety of results obtained by well-chosen materials gives distinction.

Left : The entrance to the *chaseki* is small, only about 2 ft. 7 in. square, through which the guests crawl in. They enter stripped of all the vanities of the world, leaving their rank and titles behind.

The *chaseki*, as well as *hanare* (a detached small building in the garden) is given a poetic name. Such a name helps to prepare the mind of the person who enters it. The name of this *hanare* is " Hoshintei," meaning " Truth-preserving pavilion."

A CHASEKI IN THE GARDEN OF BARON SUMITOMO, KYOTO

The stepping stones, sleeve-fences and deep eaves
bring the house close to the garden, or bring
nature close to the house.   Water-worn stones
take away from any artificial appearance and are
regarded as having a greater æsthetic value than
anything carved by man.

A narrow wooden verandah outside the rooms
seems to lead the house into the garden by
stepping stones. Home of Mr. Ohara, Kurashiki.

A CHASEKI GARDEN

A *chaseki* garden seen from the room. The panelling on the wall along the passage is of split bamboo. The pipe at the end of the eaves for draining the rain is of bamboo also. These pipes are changed for fresh ones when guests are invited.

VERANDAH, HOUSE OF MR. OHARA, KURASHIKI

A narrow extension is made to the verandah to give an access to the water-basin, which is, with the sleeve-fence, a sort of connecting link between the house and the garden. One is brought into the scene the moment one leaves the house.

WATER-BASIN AND STEPPING STONES

Tsukubai, the stone water-basin, and stepping-stones outside the *chaseki* of the Hoshigaoka Charyo, showing the intimate relation of the building with the garden.

The wall of the building on the left is covered with a fence dressed with bamboo branches. A lantern is hung from a rock half concealed by shrubbery. Note the design of paving and fence.

ENTRANCE TO A RESTAURANT, NAGOYA

The path is swept and watered, as every house in
Japan is required to be when expecting guests.

ENTRANCE TO THE HOSHIGAOKA CHARYO, TOKYO

The house is almost completely hidden among
trees, suggestive of peace and quiet within.

MR. NAKAMURA'S VILLA IN NARA

When the paper screen is pushed open, one may
have a splendid view of the garden as a living picture in a frame. The garden comes up to the
house. The small detached fences go out, as it
were, from the house to welcome the garden.

SLEEVE FENCE, HOUSE OF BARON KONDO, TOKYO

The sleeve-fence of bamboo is in perfect harmony with the framework on the underside of the eave, and with the fence in the garden, thus placing the garden in an intimate relation to the house.

Water-basin and an extension of corridor for convenience in using it. The extension is floored with bamboo, and has a railing on one side and one end left open to give access to the garden, which seems to merge into the house.

THE INTERIOR

The problem which the modern Western architect has set himself to solve has been dealt with by the Japanese in an inspiring manner. Built-in storage room, the perfection of simplicity, window-walls admitting the maximum air and light, rooms of adjustable size, are here to be found in plenty.

ROOM IN THE KŌBUNTEI, TOKIWA KŌYEN, MITO

Here is a room with framed landscape compositions on the walls, and the added advantage that you can walk into them. The paper screens slide in grooves and can be removed entirely.

BANQUET HALL IN HOTEL, SENDAI

The hall is capable of laying 225 mats, each mat measuring three by six feet. The handwriting in the frame hung over the beam means " Eternal Universe." It seems marvellous that such an expanse of ceiling can be supported on such small timbers, but the practice in Japan is to hang the whole ceiling from the ridge of the roof.

Interior of an apartment in the Chion-in temple, Kyoto, showing *fusuma* paintings of plum and pine trees under snow by a Kano artist. The austerity of the wood construction and of the plain wadded matting forms a wonderful setting for these masterpieces of painting.

RAMMA CARVING, CHIKUBUSHIMA SHRINE

A *ramma* carving in wood, " Chrysanthemums and
Pheasant," between the beams of the sixteenth-
century Chikubushima Shrine, Chikubushima, an
island in Lake Biwa. A *ramma* often serves as a
ventilating panel in a wall, and becomes a *tour de
force* in wood carving.

A scene in the *chaseki* in the course of ceremonial tea. The guests and host are making obeisance; the host is about to have his bowl of tea after the guests have been served. Home of Mr. Miyazaki, a noted tea master, in Nagoya.

Cha-no-yu in a seven-mat room. The host is about to wipe the tea caddy before taking out powdered tea from it, which he will whisk in hot water.

A scene in a *chaseki*. The hostess has prepared a bowl of tea and the head-guest is about to take the bowl across the mat between them, which becomes a sort of "no man's land." There is a basket of flowers hung on the wall of the *tokonoma*, the only decoration in the room. The beautiful utensils used for tea are carefully arranged near the kettle.

A small room of three mats and a board in the middle. The host is preparing a bowl of tea and the lady guest is about to partake of a sweet prior to drinking tea. A poem is hung on the wall of the *tokonoma* and a basket of flowers hangs from the *tokonoma* post.

A FIFTEEN-MAT ROOM, THE "TOMBO," TSUKIJI, TOKYO

A fifteen-mat room prepared for eight guests with a cushion (*zabuton*) and an arm-rest for each. The seat nearest the *toko-bashira* (*tokonoma* post) is considered to be the most honoured. The host always takes the lowest seat at the end nearest the entrance to the room.

INTERIOR OF THE HOSHIGAOKA CHARYO, TOKYO

Interior of the Hoshigaoka Charyo, Tokyo, the sliding screens partly opened, joining three rooms into one. This is a practise lately tried in the West and capable of being developed.

TOKONOMA AND SHELVES

Tokonoma (a recess for works of art) and *chigai-dana* (shelves).   The painting on the wall is by Kano-Sanraku (1559-1635). The room containing this *tokonoma* and *chigai-dana* was recently presented by Prince Kujō to the Imperial Household Museum, in the compound of which the room will be reconstructed and preserved.

ROOM IN THE VILLA OF MR. NAKAMURA, NARA

An upstairs room provided with a shallow
tokonoma with a *kakemono* and a basket of flowers.
The upper half of the sliding screens is covered
with paper, the lower half with glass.

TOKONOMA WITH ROUND AND SQUARE WINDOWS

Every room worthy of guests should have a *tokonoma*. The illustration shows an unusual *tokonoma* built, at the corner of the room, with round and square windows. Screens being removed, one could enjoy a full view of the garden beyond the wooden corridor. A calligraph—" Spring wind brings harmony "—is hung in a frame on the narrow wall over the beam which takes the grooves for the sliding screens. That is the proper place for the framed painting or calligraph.

ROOM IN THE HOUSE OF MR. K. NEZU, AOYAMA, TOKYO

This is an interior arranged for hot weather. The lightly woven reed screens allow the air to pass through the house, yet offer a certain amount of privacy, and replace the paper sliding screens. Two may be seen hanging and two rolled up.

INTERIOR, HOUSE OF MR. J. TOMITA, NAGOYA

The sliding screens between the two rooms have been removed. The effect is one of variety in simplicity, though the light fitting has proved difficult to harmonise and would be better hidden.

An atelier of a Japanese artist, whose custom it is to paint pictures laid flat on the floor. To the left may be seen an altar for Buddhist images. The late Shimomura Kwanzan is seen at work. Note the racks for brushes.

ROOM IN THE FORMER HOUSE OF MR. J. WATANABE, TOKYO

This room shows the *tokonoma* with three *kakemono* in a set. Silk cushions are on the floor and braziers for guests. There is an arrangement of pine and cabbage in the vase on the right, the vegetable being highly esteemed for decoration.

TOKONOMA IN GARDEN-HOUSE OF MR. J. TOMITA, NAGOYA

This shows an interesting type of construction, the floor of the *tokonoma* being twice the usual depth, the *chigai-dana* (shelves) on the wall at right angles to it, and the *biwa-dai* in the corner.

ROOM IN THE HOUSE OF MR. HIRAI, KYOTO

The *tokonoma* has a *kakemono* of a painting on
fan-shaped paper, a bronze incense burner on a
stand, and a vase of flowers ; a lacquered cabinet
is at the side.

" TORIMATA," HONGO, TOKYO

A shelf for flowers, which are indispensable in the decoration of Japanese rooms. Every available space is utilized for a shelf, cupboard, or a window to give a touch of beauty to the room. Interior of " Torimata," Hongo, Tokyo, designed by Mr. S. Akaishi.

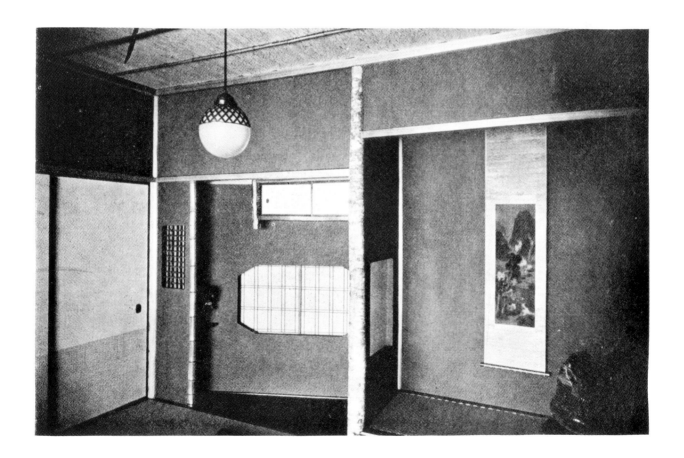

A small room ready for a *go* game (to the Western mind more complicated than chess) to be played by two persons, each provided with a brazier (for warmth) and a cushion to sit on. It is 9 ft. square, what is known as a four-and-a-half mat room, the half mat being laid at the lower right corner, and the mat next to it being cut for a hearth for boiling water. One side of the room is divided into two, for the *tokonoma* and a shelf.

A *tokonoma* in the Hoshigaoka Charyo, showing a basket of flowers hung on the wall, as is customary in the course of ceremonial tea. It is possible to study the lily and its form without irrelevant detail. For the pillar a log with natural bark is used for the sake of effect. The Japanese always allow some irregularity of this sort in an otherwise regular arrangement.

Interior of the " Tombo," Tsukiji, Tokyo. The
fusuma (sliding screens) between two rooms are
removed, joining a thirty mat room with a twelve
mat room. If occasion requires, the *shoji* (paper
screens) separating the corridors from the room
may be removed, making the hall still larger by
twenty-four mats. A pair of big braziers are shown.
Note the beautiful grain of the wood on the
ramma, simple in design.

ROOM IN THE "TOMBO," TSUKIJI, TOKYO

A room with bamboo *nageshi*, the horizontal rail, separating the upper from the lower walls. The *toko-bashira* (the *tokonoma* post) is of *cyperus rotundus*, with natural bark on.

ROOM IN THE " TOMBO," TSUKIJI, TOKYO

A room prepared for six guests, with a cushion and arm-rest for each and a brazier between two. The space next to the *tokonoma* is provided with a hanging shelf suspended from the ceiling by means of four cords, instead of being fixed to the wall.

ROOM IN THE HOUSE OF MR. MORI, TOKYO

Showing the *tokonoma* with ornaments, a low table, a brazier, *karakami* (sliding screens partitioning rooms), and *ramma* above them.

ROOM IN THE HOUSE OF MR. SHIRASU, ITAMI, OSAKA

It has a coffered ceiling, a *tokonoma* with a *kakemono* of a poem and a vase arranged with flowers, the space below the shelves being used as cupboards.

A large single board with beautiful grain of wood is used for the ceiling, surrounded by panelling. The woodwork is plain.

A CHASEKI IN THE HOSHIGAOKA CHARYO

A *chaseki* of four and a half mats. The *tokonoma*
has a wooden floor, instead of a raised floor
covered with matting.

DWELLING ROOM, JUKOIN TEMPLE, DAITOKUJI, KYOTO

Interior of the dwelling apartment of the Jukoin temple, Daitokuji, suburb of Kyoto. The sliding screens being removed, the *chaseki* is shown with a kettle in the brazier. The reproduction also shows the use made of an ordinary wall as a *tokonoma*, by hanging a *kakemono* and a basket of flowers on the wall and placing a black lacquered board on the floor.

A CHASEKI, HOUSE OF BARON KONDO, TOKYO

Showing the *daime-bashira*, the post of interesting shape rising from the corner of the hearth for the kettle. The dark space at the bottom right-hand corner is the hearth.

A CHASEKI OF FOUR AND A HALF MATS, THE "TOMBO" TSUKIJI, TOKYO

A kettle is shown in the brazier cut in the floor, and a bamboo *daime-bashira*, the post which stands at the corner of the brazier and supports a narrow wall. The *daime-bashira* is one of the most important parts of the *chaseki*. A tree with natural bark, and a curvature at about two and half feet from the floor, is generally chosen for it. Note the variety of materials used in the construction of the room, and the variation in shapes and sizes of the walls, windows and ceilings, etc.

PORCH OF THE HOUSE OF MR. NAKAMURA, NARA

The entrance to the house is roomy. Visitors may wait inside the house while the servant goes to inform the master. The entrance room is called the *genkan*, and constitutes an important feature of a Japanese home. Mr. Nakamura's home in Nara. The sandals (*geta*) are left at the entrance.

Cha-no-yu rooms designed by Katakiri Sekishu in the living quarters of the Taimadera. A very shallow *tokonoma* of uneven depth with a frame in bamboo is exceptional.

GUEST ROOM, HOUSE OF MR. YAGI, KYOTO

Guest room with *tokonoma* and shelves. Through
the glass sliding doors a full view of the garden
may be had. The picture has the place of honour.

A bell-shaped window is very effectively used in a large room here.

A flower-vase is often hung from the post. The beam (*nageshi*) supporting the narrow wall over the bell-shaped window has an auxiliary beam, and the beam over the *tokonoma* is slightly raised so that it rests on the *nageshi* (in order to avoid too great regularity of line).

TOKONOMA AND CUPBOARD

Below : A cupboard was constructed at one end of the *tokonoma*, as there is no space for shelves next to it. The hanging wall at the back of the *tokonoma* is narrower and has no beam at the bottom. Two *zabuton* (cushions) and a smoking set are put out for the guests.

Opposite : (*a*) The wall next to the *tokonoma* is sometimes left blank, and fitted only with a low cupboard built close to the window. The different levels of horizontal beams supporting the narrow walls from the ceiling are carefully studied to give a pleasing effect. The bamboo beam over the cupboard is placed slightly lower than that over the *tokonoma*, the top of one being level with the bottom of the other. The beam on the other side of the *tokonoma* is much heavier and placed lower than the others, the difference in level being about equal to the width of the bamboo beam on the opposite side. (*b*) A round window is often very effectively placed in a room. The *tokonoma* post also plays a very important part, and here a large bamboo has been used. This is an unusually shallow *tokonoma*.

TOKONOMA, KŌBUNTEI, MITO

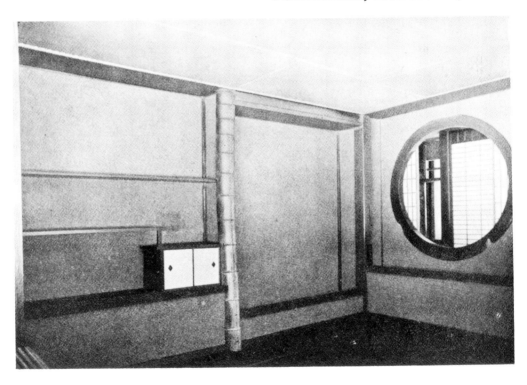

SLIDING SCREEN

The width of the sliding screens is generally the same as that of the *tatami* (mat), that is about three feet. The height of the screens (*fusuma*) in ordinary homes used always to be five and a half feet, but nowadays there is a necessary increase in height, owing to a tendency for the people to grow taller.

Tansu (chest of drawers) in a cupboard, hidden by sliding screens, which look like a partition between two rooms. The other view shows the room with the screens pushed open. The cabinet at the right is a characteristic piece of Japanese furniture made of Paiblonia wood, with black gunmetal handles.

A view of the room revealing the chest of drawers by pushing back the sliding screens. When the screens are drawn back, no one would suspect the existence of the chest.

The verandah is doubled where its course is changed, and is provided with a railing where it comes to an abrupt end and where the water basin stands. A roof is placed over the basin in autumn in order to prevent leaves from falling into it.

A guest-room with *tokonoma* and side shelves. The *zabuton* (cushions) are placed when guests are expected and they are put away when they leave. The cupboards above the shelves are generally used for keeping *kakemono*, which are changed according to the guests expected. The absence of furniture makes for restfulness.

ROOM IN THE HOUSE OF MR. NAKAMURA, NARA

A ground-floor room showing the *tokonoma* with
its side wall opening latticed with bamboo poles
of uneven height.

A *tokonoma* with a *kakemono* of a crane. The round *toko-bashira* (*tokonoma* post) has a natural surface of bark-stripped wood and the *toko-buchi* and *biwa-dai*, with the vase of flowers, are lacquered black. The different parts of the frame-work are in correct proportion to the *toko-bashira*, a very important point.

A CHASEKI INTERIOR

Interior of a *chaseki*, a room for ceremonial tea. There is infinite variety in the construction of these rooms : different kinds of wood and bamboo of various textures and surfaces being used for the posts, beams, ceiling, etc. Variety may be seen also in the shapes and sizes of the walls, thus avoiding monotony.

Cupboards and shelves for convenience in serving meals in the guest room, as the custom is. In Japanese houses the dining-room is generally for the family, meals for the guests being served in other rooms. Baron Kondo's home in Tokyo.

BATHROOM, HOUSE OF MR. YAGI, KYOTO

The bath-tub constructed of wood gives a soft and pleasing touch to the body. Often cedar wood is used giving a delightful fragrance when the bath is filled with hot water. People wash with soap, and scrub themselves, not in the tub, but outside it so that the water in the tub may be kept clean for others to use and get warmed. The tank at left is of white veined granite.

Mizuya, the room where preparations for *cha-no-yu* are made   Each object has its own place conveniently arranged and fixed.   This saves confusion and increases efficiency.

A corner of the room, with a fixed table where ornaments may be placed against the background of paper screen. A perforated design on the wooden panel over the screens is effective, as the light shines through the design. The holes also serve for ventilation.

The frame of a round window may be constructed
by bending two flexible pieces of wood with a
natural surface. The shutter may be hinged at
the top on the outside and pushed open from inside
with a stick.

JAPANESE ARCHITECTURAL TERMS USED IN THIS VOLUME

AMADO : wooden shutters to protect the outside glass doors at night.

BIWA-DAI : an alcove extension of the *tokonoma*, for the display of flower arrangements.

BUKE-ZUKURI : the *samurai* (warrior-class) style in early Japanese architecture, a modification of the *shinden-zukuri* (q.v.).

CHA-NO-YU : the tea-ceremony, which has had a far-reaching influence on all forms of art ; originally a pastime of the upper classes, but by the sixteenth century widely adopted by the common people.

CHASEKI : tea-house or room for the *cha-no-yu* ceremony (q.v.). See also : *daime-bashira, kinin-guchi, mizuya, nijiri-guchi.*

CHIGAI-DANA : shelves at uneven levels in an alcove, the *toko-waki* (q.v.), adjoining the *tokonoma.*

CHOZUBACHI : a stone basin outside the house for washing hands and rinsing mouth, usually by the verandah overlooking the garden. Water is taken from it with a long-handled dipper. Also called *tsukubai.*

DAIME-BASHIRA : a post of natural shape situated at the corner of the sunken hearth in the *chaseki*, supporting a narrow curtain wall.

EN : a long fixed wooden bench, either inside or outside the house.

FUSUMA : panels formed of a wooden framework covered with decorated paper on both sides, and used as a sliding screen between rooms. See *shoin-zukuri.*

GENKAN : the entrance, generally comprising an antechamber where shoes are removed, with a sheltered extension for vehicles. A house usually has two entrances, the *omote-genkan* for guests, and the *nai-genkan*, a side entrance for the family. See *shoin-zukuri.*

HANARE : a small detached pavilion in the garden.

HOGYO : a roof radiating in four or more directions from one point, without a ridge-pole.

IRIMOYA : a form of roof in two sections, the upper with gables like the *kirizuma*, and the lower with surfaces as in the *shichu.*

KAERU-MATA : decorative supports to beams.

KAKEMONO : rolled painting (picture or calligraph) on silk, such as is hung in the *tokonoma.*

KAMOI : the deeply grooved upper beam which holds a sliding partition. See also *shikii.*

KARAKAMI : sliding screens partitioning rooms.

KEN : a unit of measurement of about 6 ft.

KININ-GUCHI : a side of the *chaseki* so constructed that it may be opened wide for the entry of important persons.

KIRIZUMA : the gable form of roof.

KONDO : main sanctuary of a temple.

KUTSUNUGI-ISHI (shoe-removing stone) : a foot-rest outside the entrance to a house, for the removal of shoes before entering.

MISU : a curtain made of split bamboo or reeds, hung from a beam, and replacing during the summer months the *fusuma* and *shoji* (qq.v.).

MIZUYA (water-room) : the room where preparations are made for the tea-ceremony.

NAGESHI : a horizontal beam separating the upper and lower parts of a wall.

NIJIRI-GUCHI : a small square window-like entrance to the ceremonial tea room, to enter which one has to kneel, a sign that rank and station are set aside.

OTOSHIGAKE : the beam supporting the narrow overhanging wall across the top front of the *tokonoma.*

RAMMA : a panel fitted between the beam above the partitions of rooms and the ceiling, carved, and often fretted for ventilation ; sometimes made to slide open and shut.

SHICHU (or *yosemune*) : a form of roof sloping away from the ridge-pole on four sides, without forming gables.

SHIKII : the lower grooved beam upon which the partitions slide. See *kamoi.*

SHINDEN-ZUKURI : a style of architecture developed by the aristocracy in the tenth century A.D. (see page 19).

SHOIN-ZUKURI : a development of the *buke* style of architecture, responsible for the introduction of the *tokonoma, fusuma, sugito* and *genkan* (qq.v.). Also the room containing the *tokonoma* and its dependent features.

SHOJI : sliding screen covered on one side only with white paper, in order to admit light. See *fusuma.*

SODE-GAKI : an ornamental " sleeve " fence, projecting from the house to the garden, and helping to establish a connection between the two.

SUGITO : wooden panelled doors, with or without decoration. See *shoin-zukuri.*

TANSU : chest of drawers or bureau.

TATAMI : wadded mats (rice straw covered with reed matting) of standard dimensions, covering the whole floor of a room, and adopted as units of measurement ; introduced in the fifteenth century.

TENJO : ceiling.

TOKO-BASHIRA : the post separating the *tokonoma* and the *toko-waki*, the chief pillar in the house.

TOKO-BUCHI : see *toko-kamachi.*

TOKO-KAMACHI : the piece of wood completing the lower front of the *tokonoma*, to the level of which the floor within is raised. Also called *toko-buchi.*

TOKO-WAKI (*tokonoma* side) : an alcove adjoining the *tokonoma*, containing *chigai-dana* (shelves of uneven lengths) and small cupboards with sliding doors.

TOKONOMA : a recess with a raised floor in the main guest-chamber, or in the *chaseki*, for a poem or painting (*kakemono*), or a flower arrangement, or both. It is the place of honour in the room in which it is situated. See also *otoshigake, shoin-zukuri, toko-bashira, toko-kamachi, toko-waki.*

TORII : the symbol of a Buddhist or Shinto shrine ; two horizontal beams supported by two posts, in its simplest form.

TSUBO : a unit of surface measurement, the space occupied by two *tatami* (q.v.) ; about 6 ft. square.

TSUKI-AGE MADO : a skylight with a movable cover.

TSUKUBAI : see *chozubachi.*

YOSEMUNE : see *shichu.*

ZABUTON : cushion seat on the floor.